CW00386274

REMOTE V
SENSING FC

REMOTE VIEWING AND SENSING FOR MANAGERS

*How to Use Military Psiops
for a Competitive Edge*

Tim Rifat

The author would like to thank all at Vision Paperbacks for their help and support.

First published in Great Britain in 2003 by Vision Paperbacks,
a division of Satin Publications Ltd.
101 Southwark Street
London SE1 0JF
UK
info@visionpaperbacks.co.uk
www.visionpaperbacks.co.uk
Publisher: Sheena Dewan

A catalogue record for this book
is available from the British Library.

ISBN: 1-904132-31-6

2 4 6 8 10 9 7 5 3 1

Typeset by M Rules
Printed and bound in the UK by
Mackays of Chatham Ltd, Chatham, Kent

CONTENTS

ONE

OVERVIEW OF PSIOPS MANAGEMENT

The development of remote viewing and sensing by both superpowers during the cold war was a purely military endeavour. As the only non-military expert on this psychic spying I was unconstrained by national security, and hence free to write a textbook on the subject (*Remote Viewing: Who does it, Why it works and How to do it*, Vision Paperbacks 2001).

Remote Viewing (RV) is the ability to psychically view distant locations, such as top secret military bases. Remote Sensing (RS) is, as I will explain in what follows, the ability to psychically scan the minds of target individuals. Trained remote sensors have the capacity to scan the minds of enemy intelligence heads, generals and decision makers. As one may appreciate, this is not the type of technology a CIA or DIA 'retired' agent would reveal to the public. I have written this book to show people how remote viewing and sensing can be used in the business environment. Not only can one develop empathy to better understand the feelings of one's staff so as to better motivate them, one can also telepathically scan one's competitors' minds to learn their secrets.

I have named the use of remote viewing and remote sensing in business 'psiops management'. This is an evolution of PSYOPS – the manipulation of the public and enemy minds by disinformation, psychological tricks and inside knowledge – the forte of the US military. The *New York Times* (and other sources) reported that the Pentagon had a special department responsible for misinforming the news media. In this book, the reader is introduced to all aspects of psiops and develops the psychological technology to encompass the psi-world. It addresses the basics of remote viewing – the stress management system so important to psi-work – and for the first time gives the detailed protocols of remote sensing in a business context.

The practicalities of remote sensing and remote viewing

Remote viewing is almost unknown in humans. This is because stress-related phenomena switch off the psi-genes. Stress therefore interferes with the mechanism of RV and RS. It is vital that the high levels of stress and anxiety found in the normal person be lowered for any paranormal phenomenon to occur. This process of activating RV abilities must reduce the high levels of neurohormones and the blizzard of electrical over-stimulation of the nervous system which blinds us to RV and RS. In the business scenario, stress is a normal penalty of overwork. Burnout is common in our most successful executives. Understanding the processes that control stress enables the psiops manager to thrive on it, increases her or his efficiency and activates psi-abilities.

Ways of activating RV and RS must therefore address ways of making the subject deeply relaxed. Many thousands of years ago, meditation was created to lower our basal stress levels. This came about as our predecessors discovered by a method of trial and error that stress interferes with all parapsychological activity. By this same method of trial and error, our ancestors learnt how to inculcate states of consciousness that were conducive to paranormal activity. In modern times, these ancient systems of meditation are still being used, for we lack modern techniques to bring about the same states.

Major Ed Dames, the renowned former US military remote viewer, stated in one of his speeches that: 'remote viewers appear to be in the theta state of consciousness while they are carrying out RV.' Theta is the state of consciousness normally associated with the dreaming state, lucid dreaming and projection. It is defined as registering 4–7 cycles per second on EEG machines, and can be induced by biofeedback to occur while conscious. (An EEG machine – or electroencephalogram – tests electrical changes from nerve cells in the brain.)

The US military's programme of RV development takes at least a year of study before adequate results are obtained. Criteria of efficiency being, according to Joe McMoneagle (a former US Army Special Projects Intelligence remote viewer), the ability to get the target (the general area he is supposed to be viewing) about 25–28 per cent of the time. Once on target, an average 85 per cent of the information gleaned will be correct.

This year of study and training is necessary because the brain takes that long to settle down into a basal theta state with the primitive parapsychological technology at their disposal. Accelerated RV therefore requires a shortcut to lowering brain stress levels and, as a result, brain rhythms.

My research has led me to conclude that there are two main factors which elevate human stress levels: the over-stimulation of the brain stress system and the acquisition of negative memes that degrade parapsychological performance. Memes include ideas and habitual ways of acting and functioning that are passed on as mental software; an example is driving a car. They are acquired software which mould our neural networks in unique ways; for instance speaking a language, table manners, etc. These two factors may be new to some readers and will be discussed later.

Research into ways of advancing our knowledge of stress management systems must deal with these two factors, so that the basal stress level of the operative is naturally reduced to the theta level. By doing this, we have opened up a pathway to an accelerated method of learning RV and RS techniques. A welcome by-product of this practice of stress-management-mediated RV and RS causes a marked improvement in physiological and mental functioning in people using this training.

This is because RV and RS phenomena only occur when the brain is in a quiescent state – normally found when the subject is deeply meditative. This is also optimal for boosting the immune system and suppressing psychosomatic disease. Because it switches off the body's habituated state of electrical over-stimulation and the sea of stress-inducing neurochemicals – which induce cancer, mental problems, heart disease and a whole range of psychosomatic diseases – the brain state that is needed for RV and RS also boosts lifespan and makes the practitioner much more resistant to disease.

Even when this process has been achieved, large amounts of interference will still be noticed by the RV/RS operator. This is because our mental processes are locked into negative feedback cycles that severely degrade our ability to function appropriately. These negative software programmes and

memes that afflict humanity are reinforced by the organisations we work within; these communities of managers and
staff endlessly externalise these negative programmes in the
work place. Organisations therefore suffer from the human
stress disease and all its associated memes, but on a grander
scale.

Our society seems as though it were designed not only
to block out all RV and RS activity, but also to make us
perform poorly at work, age us at an accelerated rate and
make us susceptible to psychosomatic disease. In fact 90
per cent of all western diseases are psychosomatically
induced; cancer is the most notorious example. Backing
up this devastating effect of the modern person's milieu of
anxiety and stress is an accelerated rate of scientific and
technical advancement that is leaving the individual feeling
inadequate and 'shell shocked'. One result of this is that
more Americans die of cancer now than they did in the
1970s, despite a concerted multi-billion dollar campaign by
the US government to cure cancer.

We are now falling victim to cancers at an accelerated
rate. Mortality, generally, is also up. Our modern milieu is
a stress-inducing, anxiety-ridden world, where all of us are
being continually forced beyond our physical and psychological limits. No wonder RV and RS are almost
unknown in the general population. The high basal stress
levels of western people release a torrent of neurohormonal and electrical stimuli that not only appears to switch
off the psi-genes, but also switches on the oncogenes that
cause cancer. This means that paranormal phenomena are
rare in the general population and lack the repeatability
needed for scientific verification.

Defining psiops management

Psiops management consists of the use of military research into how remote viewing and sensing work and how the mind can be used to psychically spy, and its application to promoting the creative power that lies hidden in individuals. These psi-abilities – such as clairvoyance, extra sensory perception (ESP) and mind over matter – were systematically developed by the superpowers for use in a Third World War. The author has applied these top secret protocols of psi-warfare to management science, in the process generating an offshoot of this called psiops management. This is a science of management derived from research into remote viewing (psychic spying) and associated paranormal warfare techniques developed by the superpowers at the height of the Cold War. I have refined those that are applicable to the business world and made them accessible to civilians.

Overview of military psiops relevant to managers

Psiops management was developed by the superpowers to explore the military strategic and tactical use of ESP and related phenomena. The simplest of these techniques was remote viewing, whereby US and Soviet personnel were trained in psychic espionage. One consequence of this research has been the establishment of a body of knowledge about the human brain and related aspects of human performance, but this is unknown outside US and Russian military circles. In Europe, virtually nothing is known about these developments, and the author is the only recognised expert in the EU with expertise in these psiops techniques on a par with that of current serving Russian and US military practitioners.

Psiops management is based upon an overview of the

scientific research into brain functioning relevant to civilian and business applications. This technology opens a new vista in management science, as the results of this military domain research (independently developed by the author) offer ways of dramatically improving the profitability of business people by enhancing their performance. There are four main areas of findings which are described in this book:

1. State-of-the-art stress management systems

Psiops management trains the operator to enter the deep condition of relaxation called the theta state which is, as discussed, normally found in dreaming. I have developed a technique for lowering stress levels in personnel to enable them to function optimally. This stress management system can enhance the mental and physical efficiency of people by a factor of four. It also eliminates the free-floating anxiety which pervades many people, and will inculcate a positive outlook. Attitude is also synergistically improved as the person is in the optimum mental state even under stress.

2. Developing real-time outlook

Decreasing the resistance to change in a person is necessary if she or he is to keep up with the fast-moving world situation. Psiops management research has enabled me to pinpoint the key rate-limiting steps in achieving a real-time outlook that can thrive on change. Most people need too long to respond to any significant change in market conditions. Organisations using the techniques being presented can change quickly in response to events and therefore out-react their competitors. This radically improves the person or organisation's profitability in difficult times, and also enables them to make the best use of management techniques to cope with the fast-moving pace of survival in the post-9/11 maelstrom of war.

3. Enhancing performance

This book has used the results of military science research into psi to develop techniques for dramatically improving all areas of mental performance. This technology can enable people to boost their intelligence, memory, extrapolative skills, creative thinking and ability to construct mental simulations of the business milieu and plan strategically. Further to this, the results of psiops management research can show people how to increase the stamina and fitness of their minds and bodies to the point that they can actually thrive on stress. Since a company depends on its managers to guide it to success, augmenting the performance of the human component of an organisation will boost the profitability of all areas of its core competency. Remote viewing, as we will see later, enables the practitioner to psychically spy on the world situation, so one is never in the dark as to the intentions of competitive businesses.

4. Entering the mindset of your competitors

Psiops management research is based on remote viewing and sensing, which was designed to be used to discover the enemy's intentions during the Cold War. Management science applications of this remote viewing technology enable users of this book to psychically spy on organisations and simulate the mindsets of their competitors. Being able to judge what business rivals will do, a manager can steer company policy to make best use of this knowledge, blocking competitors from achieving their goals and boosting their own organisation's profitability in the process. Related to this are remote sensing techniques and the military use of ESP, which can be used to develop intuition and the so-called gut feeling in managers. Remote sensing can also be used by staff who are well versed in psiops management research to see into the mind of rivals. This results in an organisation that can outguess its competitors as well as out-think them.

Stress management systems which increase the human performance envelope

Since remote viewing and sensing require the operator to work in the theta state, it is now clear why I had to develop powerful techniques and methodology to inculcate lowered basal stress levels. In fact this book describes one of the most powerful stress reduction systems in existence. It can now be seen why a state-of-the-art stress reduction system was developed to reduce the antagonistic stressors that were switching off the psi-genes needed for RV and RS. It also became apparent that these techniques would be applicable to organisations and their managers and staff, who were driven into high states of anxiety by their jobs. This stress-reduction system not only enhances RV and RS capacity, it also enables:

- Increased memory capacity, retention of data in short-term memory and retrieval of this data from the long-term memory.

- Enhanced stamina, due to the body not requiring as much energy to run itself in an unstressed state, as opposed to the normal stressed-out state.

- Boosted mental capacity; in the order of two to four times that found in normally stressed individuals.

- The ability to think ahead and formulate mental simulations of enormous complexity.

- More efficient use of one's latent intelligence.

- A large increase in the intuitive capacity of the person, leading to successful hunches.

Further to this, the author found it was necessary to optimise the memes people had acquired. It was found that a considerable number of the memes we had acquired throughout our lives degraded RV and RS capability – the intuitive hunches that bring fortune. As I mentioned previously, memes can be seen as acquired software which mould our neural networks in unique ways. For RV and RS activity, a listing of all the negative memes is needed so they can be eradicated, freeing up the biophysical energy needed for remote viewing and sensing.

Nature abhors a vacuum, so negative memes will resurface unless they are replaced by positive memes. I have designed a set of simple positive memes which enhance RV and RS. A knock-on effect of utilising these memes is that they enhance human potential, enabling the person using them to better development of their latent abilities. These positive memes also reduce the basal level of the stress neurohormones and their associated electrical activity. This results in a technology that enable the RV and RS operator to control their reaction to stress, such that they can thrive in an environment that would make normal people physical and mental wrecks.

Stress reduction for RV

Let us first look at the stress-related processes going on within people, that make RV and RS so difficult for the brain stress system.

Within the brain, old and new structures are incorporated into a mechanism by which the organism can respond to stress. Brain structure is linked to old 'reptilian' structures in the brain stem. It is from these ancient neurological systems that underpin our higher brain structure, that other more advanced areas have developed.

The reptilian brain stem structures have evolved in such a way that they are now enclosed by the limbic system (which consists of the thalamus, hypothalamus and amygdala – see glossary) and surrounding this, the cortex. These three major brain structures are intimately connected to each other. Their interaction controls our state of stress. This system is activated by any stimulus that is seen to be threatening. New memes like RV and RS have a similar effect on our brain stress system (see glossary). There is an instinctive fear of parapsychological phenomena, as they upset the ordered world view that we all cling to.

How does this stress mediated physiological degradation of our paranormal abilities occur? It begins with an ancient brain structure, the *locus coeruleus*, which is part of the brain stem – the so-called reptilian brain. The brain stem, and hence the *locus coeruleus*, is the underpinning of our consciousness and awareness. Our brain stem is hardwired to respond to reptilian memes of dominance, pecking order and such like. The *locus coeruleus* initiates the brain stress system when the pecking order of dominance over inferiors and submission to superiors is disrupted. Ritualistic behaviour and adherence to the status quo are some of the chief factors that keep the reptilian brain from activating our brain stress system. Belief in one's leaders and the shared and ineffaceable idea of the material world being the only reality can also be included.

The net effect of the above factors is to reduce over-stim-ulation of the brain stress system. In the modern world, our milieu's uncertain nature undermines all the above factors, and this reduces the amount of stimulation needed to activate the *locus coeruleus*. Since this structure is intimately related to 'detonation' of the brain stress system, modern man is in a perpetual state of stress.

One can now see the importance of enlarging the world view to include parapsychological phenomena as extensions of science, as this raises the threshold of the onset of stress within the person so affected. A detailed explanation of RV/RS is therefore needed, not so people can understand the intricacies of the mechanisms involved, but so that their world view is not shattered with the concomitant elevation of basal stress rates that shut down paranormal activity.

This principle gives us the first law of RV and RS:

---

1. Effective RV/RS must augment the world view by extending the common consensus of what is possible, to include the paranormal.

Science is the best tool for that purpose, as we can then include paranormal phenomena as a branch of biophysics which we are now just beginning to understand. Conversely, to develop RV/RS, we must avoid things which activate the *locus coeruleus*. These stressors are:

- Poorly defined linguistic and ideational structures, upon

which the pupil finds it impossible to impose order such that these new phenomena can be assimilated into their own mental organisations of reality. A prime example of this is the subjective descriptions and the occult language that psychics use to describe paranormal phenomena. This non-scientific description of reality may be based on fact, but conventional scientists find it impossible to decode in a way that is applicable to conventional science.

- Phenomena that the pupil sees conflict with common sense. An example of this might be the idea that witches fly on broomsticks – which we know have all the aero-dynamic properties of a brick.

- New ways of thinking that lower people's images of themselves by making them feel like idiots. Many so-called 'new age' techniques try to lower the self-esteem of participants so they can be brainwashed into accepting the tenets of the cult. These cults are therefore good means of shutting down RV phenomena in their followers.

This gives us the second law of RV and RS:

2. The practice of RV and RS must be seen to enhance the self-importance of the pupil by showing them that they have the potential to be superhuman.

Self-importance is a characteristic which directly addresses the reptilian part of the brain. Dominance and pecking order are an integral part of the reptilian brain's programming. Anything which elevates the self-importance of the person will reduce the brain stress system's anxiety and will therefore make the person feel good. If you stimulate people's self-importance by showing them they can experience all areas of RV/RS, this will cause a positive reaction in the person. Every time they remember RV/RS, they will relive this pleasurable state that was initiated in them. This means there will be positive feedback when RV/RS is practised, which makes people willing and able to implement the things they learnt about in the RV/RS course.

These RV/RS memes will then be passed through organisations by fellow workers copying the assured and optimal behaviour demonstrated by the RV/RS operator in the workplace. This behaviour was designed to raise their self-importance. These simple principles are as follows:

- Give deference to your superiors, make them feel they are higher up the pecking order, without being sycophantic.

- Treat your staff as equals, but at the same time let them know the final say is yours.

- Have regular meetings where, at your insistence, your juniors can give valid feedback on the pros and cons of your ideas and where they are asked to help optimise your stratagems. This allows you to obtain realistic feedback, without your juniors feeling they would insult you if they told you the truth. You save face and gain respect because you are admitting your ideas are not perfect and are man or woman enough to ask their advice. Secondly, you are massaging their self-importance, as you are bringing them into management decisions.

Thirdly, once you have agreed upon a course of action it is more likely to be better implemented as everyone has been included.

- Inculcate this behaviour down the chain of command.

- Make it department and company policy to have feedback sessions from the highest to the lowest members of the organisation, as this builds team spirit.

This is all standard management science, which many readers will be aware of. The new idea is that to develop RV/RS skills, the workplace must be used as a means to habitually inculcate new memes that lower the basal level of the brain stress system and therefore boost paranormal abilities. We spend most of our productive time at work, so it is necessary to use the work environment to habituate oneself to RV/RS methodology. In the process, one gets better at the job and leaves work feeling less tired. Carrying out the above actions also means people will be more likely to follow one's ideas and pursue one's wishes.

Continuing our discussion of the brain stress system, the *locus coeruleus* sends signals, chemical and otherwise, to the hypothalamus which is part of the limbic system. Emotional drives and urges are centred in the limbic system, the hippocampus, which is intimately related with data retrieval and storage, and the thalamus, which is posited as the organ of attention. Anxiety and the level of activity of the brain stress system, therefore, have an immense effect on the way RV/RS and associated material are attended to, acted upon, then remembered and retrieved when needed. Anything which ameliorates the high levels of chemical and electrical over-stimulation found in anxious people will have profound effects on RV/RS mentation and related data acquisition and retrieval in the person. It will also boost intelligence and memory in the RV/RS operator.

In the next section, we deal with some of the fundamental principles of ESP that not only switch off stressed states, but turn on positive states when data from the psychic scanning of other people is retrieved. This is what I call remote sensing.

TWO

REMOTE SENSING: THE AXIOMS OF RS

The goal is to manifest the true potential within yourself. To accomplish this we need: the Axioms of RS:

————

1. The person's perception of her/himself is incomplete due to filtering by the brain and imprinting by our environment of negative programmes which compete with and warp proper perception: **An RS operator sees only the total reality of his or her self**. It is a sad fact that we carry a number of memes that specifically cut off all paranormal functioning.

————

2. Our perception affects reality and vice versa. **An RS operator lives in total reality**. This is a state of perfect perception where reality is not compromised by negative programming and preconceptions about how you think you are. These negative memes reconfigure the neural networks in our brain to block out all paranormal phenomena.

————

3. Group consciousness defines group reality. **An RS operator can step outside of group perception and hence group reality**. Memes not only warp the neural networks but re-programme the latent biophysical fields so that they are crippled.

————

How we get to this goal is what this book is all about. I wish to show you that the magic key to success is knowledge of the biophysics of RS. Once you can perceive unfiltered reality, with no preconceptions about what you can and cannot do, then you are able to leave the common consensus. Having stepped outside the flow of group consciousness, you can begin to appreciate hidden potentials. RS is then available to the individual. To know the true you, and how you can use your abilities, is the goal of RS.

As an introductory exercise, you should relax. In your mind's eye, imagine your awareness fixated on your brain. Visualise the three different areas of the brain – the cortex, limbic system and 'reptilian' brain stem areas – as three concentric circles, with the reptilian brain in the middle, joined to your spinal cord. Visualise your biophysical field becoming stronger and 'soaking' into the brain, linking with the neural nets by use of calcium efflux effects. This process primes the biophysical fields to interact with your brain on a higher level than morphogenetic effects.

Visualise an energy field which overlays your body, the biophysical field that is contiguous with your physical being, becoming imprinted with the three axioms of RS. Intend this biophysical field commanding your brain centres to become compliant with the three axioms, preparing your brain for remote sensing activity.

This technique of programming the biophysical field is very important in that it is used to programme the specific brain centres for remote sensing as described in later chapters. Biophysical fields carry information and they can be programmed just like a computer. The biophysical field is really a quantum computer.

The mechanism of RS

We can, in fact, change all aspects of our performance thus being able to have the edge over all our competitors. The first step is to list the perceptual cues we get when we try and remotely sense a person of interest, eg:

Visual	* medium height
	* long blonde hair
Sonic	* high pitched voice
Tactile	* curvaceous
	* soft
Empathic	* feminine
	* light and flighty
	* nurturing
Intellectual	* normal intellect
	* worldly wise

Thus we can list the attributes of our remotely-sensed person, so we can build a picture in our mind's eye of what that person is, and the emotional and mental state they are in, as well as their core emotional and intellectual components. In the above case, the person we were remotely sensing was the archetype of western man's female dream mate – as influenced by the media.

As an exercise, imagine a person you know. Keep repeating this distant visualisation of actual people you know. This exercise trains your biophysical awareness to remotely sense other people. It also raises the biophysical awareness from morphogenetic field functions to primary awareness. In plain language, you are training your biophysical fields to becoming aware of the biophysical fields of other people. The morphogenetic field is the body's biophysical field which controls and co-ordinates your cells to function as one. With training one can energise this field and make it self-aware, a necessary prerequisite for RS. This state is called primary awareness.

For a second exercise, we start training our biophysical awareness to visualise people we know well, such as close relatives or lovers. We keep a log of our RS, and begin to check on our sensings, asking people the emotional state they were in when we remotely sensed them; this information can then be checked against what we remotely sensed. The end result of this training is that we can remotely sense their location and state of mind – we can train our biophysical awareness to seek them out.

In the third exercise we remotely sense people we know while we know where they are and then we can ring them up to see whether we were correct. In carrying out this technique, the remote senser looks for glowing shapes, which is the energy field given off by the person. This is a preliminary exercise which develops the bifunctional sensing capacity of our RS biophysical field effects. This means that our RS perception can sense people as physical objects or can look at their biophysical or psychotronic aspects. In the realm of RS, perception is a duality analogous to the particle wave duality found in quantum mechanics. Later we will explore this concept in more detail.

In remote sensing it is important to match the biophysical field of the person you are remotely sensing, so to do this, visualise your own biophysical field and match its intensity and colour plus size and feeling, with the biophysical field of the person you are remotely sensing. The closer the alignment between your field and the person you are remotely sensing, the better the transfer of information from the person.

Psiops management applications: real-time functioning

There is a growing need for real-time control in the management of organisations. The world is becoming increasingly unstable with the 'war on terror' escalating. The accelerating pace of technological development, the information explosion, political and economic instability, resource depletion and environmental problems are combining to produce an increasing rate of change. Nothing can be taken for granted, and it is obvious that companies and other organisations must adapt to change as quickly as possible.

Ideally, an organisation would react immediately. Initiatives from management would be implemented as soon as they were passed down the chain of command. In practice, things are very different. Faced with mounting losses, some of the big multinational companies have tried restructuring, re-financing and reorganising, yet found that they could do nothing to change the attitudes, mindsets and perceptions of their staff – upon which all the new initiatives ultimately depended. We need look no further to understand how it is that once prestigious multinational giants have produced record-breaking losses. Enron collapsed, McDonalds was forced to change the burgers it sells, Ford had to rethink its business . . . No doubt you have come across the problem yourself.

In the past, when events moved slowly, organisational inertia was only rarely disastrous. Usually, there was plenty of latitude and mistakes could be got away with for years on end. Today, however, that latitude has gone and organisations which cannot adapt quickly are on the path to oblivion.

Yet even organisations that are willing to accept and embrace change find it difficult to adapt. Research has shown that it takes, on average, three years to alter the working practices and attitudes of staff in a large organisation, and no less than ten years in institutions. But in an unstable world, a three-year reaction time to external conditions leaves the organisation totally out of step with current events. It is then necessary to rely on accurate forecasts to judge, for example, which products are unprofitable and should be dropped. Unfortunately, organisations which follow strategies relying on accurate forecasting lay themselves open to making decisions which later prove wrong. A common example relates to established brand names, which have often been dropped, or tampered with to disastrous effect, or sold off, to make large profits under new ownership.

The constant need to look three years ahead places an increasing burden on management and those responsible for strategic planning. Managers find themselves under stress as they attempt to keep up with events: their judgement might become impaired, they are liable to become less efficient at anticipating future probabilities and can lose control. And in a chaotic world, where prediction is becoming increasingly difficult, organisations can find themselves permanently at the mercy of events.

The state of affairs which has just been described will be familiar to anyone with experience of management in industry, commerce or the public sector. In response to the problem, a variety of management techniques has burgeoned in recent years. Many of these, however, are easier said than done, and can exacerbate the difficulties by making people feel anxious and inadequate.

The methods proposed in this book adopt precisely the opposite approach. Remote viewing and sensing can enable the manager to psychically spy on events which have a bearing on the course of business within their firm. As you have seen in this chapter, the RS protocols help the psiops manager to psychically see and sense what is happening to the company in real-time. In later chapters we build on empathic awareness and give the reader the full set of RV/RS tools to accomplish this.

These sets of techniques can reduce the implementation time of management initiatives and strategies to a matter of months. They can also speed up the assimilation of company training programmes, with beneficial effects on the organisation and its profitability. The eventual aim of all these remote viewing based techniques, taken together, is to achieve real-time functioning – psiops management incorporates these to empower a company and its employees to gain immediate apprehension and response to events. Psiops management has been developed from a systematic and scientific overview of the best that the 'black budget' US military has to offer for implementing and managing change.

The methods described are best studied and applied over and over again, until they become second nature. Managers and staff then develop the ability to respond to change ever more swiftly. As this new attitude and mindset is propagated down the chain of command, the organisation itself becomes more efficient and responsive. The specific protocols for remote viewing and sensing which synergistically amplify and empower psiops management become part of company culture.

THREE

REMOTE SENSING IN ACTION

You will have found in the preliminary exercises in the previous chapter that accuracy can be a problem. Ingo Swann, the famous remote viewer, employed by the US government, has stated that in untrained people, an accuracy of 15 per cent is normal. In your RS, if you improved on this accuracy, it shows you have a greater than normal complement of psi-genes. For the rest of us, to improve accuracy we must address the problem of stress that interferes with the biophysical awareness of RS.

As mentioned previously, stress causes chaotic attention, it destroys the RS potential, as well as negating mental efficiency and increasing the entropy of the biophysical system. So important is the subject of stress control, that we have looked at the brain stress system to see how stress is generated and entrainment of theta brain rhythms.

Body and mind are obviously linked, and chaos and separation in this interface cause disease and block all RS. Management and business follow the same principle. Business success depends on a transparent interface, and this is affected by the corporate self-image (the summated programmes of the company: the Supraprogramme) which is the synthesis of the personal programmes within the personnel who make up the company.

The first step is to optimise one's personal suprapro-gramme – self-image – and to change ones reaction to environmental stimuli, to cut out chaos and entropic decay. (Entopic decay is the property of reality such that every-thing becomes more disordered unless energy and information are added to the system.)

In this exercise, relax, and visualise yourself. In your mind's eye, begin to list your characteristics and emotional reactions to situations. This exercise is important because it raises your biophysical fields from morphogenetic func-tioning to primary awareness. In this process, these fields become aware of you. It is also vital for the memetic tech-nology – which is used to rid your being of the numerous memes that make humans so limited in their capabilities that we cannot even remotely sense like our hunter–gath-erer ancestors did – that we become aware of these mental programmes so they can be optimised.

The next step is to constantly monitor your emotional and mental state throughout the day, especially while at work. Become aware of how other people can affect your emotional and mental states. After this try to sense what your workmates and friends are feeling like when you meet them. At first you may get only fleeting clues but with prac-tise you will find you become more and more aware of what mental and emotional state they are really in. This exercise develops empathic awareness – the first stage of remote sensing. In business, being aware of the true intentions and feelings of the people you deal with is very important.

In the next exercise, begin to re-programme your memes so that you can empathically sense. This is done by listing what you wish to be and what you do not wish to be. You can then enter the theta state and imagine yourself as you wish to be, systematically scrubbing away images of what you do not wish to be – reality should not impinge on this process. In psi-space you can be anyone you really wish to be. Psi-space is the mental world we all inhabit, rather like the cyberspace of the Internet.

By learning more about your own mental and emotional state, it becomes easier to remotely sense what other people are thinking and feeling. Repeat the above exercise on emotional and mental sensing of friends and workmates and you will see that the clearer your emotional and mental state, the easier it is to sense the emotional and mental states of others. This introduces us to the idea that memes, which have up until now been hidden from perception, obstruct our remote sensing abilities. Later, a discussion of RS memetics will explore this in great detail.

In the next exercise, begin to visualise that you have the ability to be aware of using your biophysical fields. Be aware that you can project them outside your body and that they can be aware of people in distant locations. In later chapters we will see how these latent biophysical field effects can be amplified to primary awareness, then the high-order consciousness of remote sensing.

For this exercise, you should acquire CDs of baroque music. This music was composed to a very rhythmic beat that entrains the brain automatically into the alpha state. The Eastern Bloc parapsychological researchers into RV and superlearning discovered that this slow, repetitive and rhythmic music naturally brought the listener into the alpha state.

Once you have these baroque music collections, play the music while you repeat the exercises just given. Note how the efficiency of your RS improves and it is easier to contact the biophysical fields. Baroque music entrainment develops neural networks which are alpha functioning (relaxed states of mind) and by a process of positive feedback, leads the RS operator's brain to be hardwired in a different way. It is as if the music moulds the brain to function in the alpha state. This state is the same as the 'daydreaming' state.

This brings us to the first rule of remote sensing:

The lower the brainwaves which are present in the brain, the more optimal the functioning to the biophysical field.

This is because the lower the brain frequencies, the more biophysical energy that is available for RS. You can try listening to baroque music on a Walkman while travelling around town, and remotely sensing the people you find of interest as they pass by. Notice how the alpha entrainment boosts RS.

Practise remote viewing

Here are some useful protocols to start up simple remote sensing by switching off the stress memes and brain over-stimulation that is considered normal. The first ones allow you to visualise your own body by directing your biophysical field to scan yourself rather than another person. As we have learnt, biophysical fields carry information. In the first step we are going to transfer information from your biophysical fields into your physical body.

1. First, relax your body. Command yourself to operate in theta whenever RS.

2. Next intend your genes to augment psi-ability. Erase all

negative oncogene activity. Do this simply by willing it (later I give detailed protocols).

3. From there, intend your body to operate in an augmented manner as listed above; in later chapters I will explain how intense interest increases RS ability by changing brain functions.

4. With the baroque music playing in the background, entrainment of an alpha state will ensue. This will facilitate your RS of any site of interest.

For the next set of protocols, pick a person that interests you, and begin to look for anything that catches the attention of your biophysical awareness. Keep a log of your RS and see how it progresses as you learn more and more techniques to boost it. In the next chapter, we are going to look at biophysical amplification. By this methodology, we can begin to raise the efficiency of RS from the 15 per cent average predicted for untrained operators.

Use the previous introductory exercises as a simple formula to follow when carrying out basic RS:

1. For practise, first use RS to sense a person in their house, then phone them up to see how effective you were.

2. Next, ask a friend to project an emotion and use RS to empathically sense what it is going on in your friend's being.

3. From there use RS to scan what your friends are think-

ing about, look for emotional and mental details you can check later with them.

4. Use RS to look for strange phenomena in people you know or see on TV. This may be a good time to look for illness in people or detecting foreign energy fields buried in people's biophysical fields. This is a useful introduction to using RS for scanning people for health problems, which we will discuss at length later.

From here, begin to use RS memes for augmented business functioning. The first step is to rigorously practise empathic awareness on everyone at work to reinforce your RS development by habituation. Practise all these memes at work and use RS to scan the emotions and intentions of your workmates. Next, use RS to scan their mental and emotional reactions to each other and you. You will find there are dramatic changes in both the emotional and mental states of yourself and your fellow workers with every interaction. Now see the effect of using the memes to boost the self-importance of your workmates. Scan them empathically to see the positive effects on them. These trivial memes have tremendous power. Imagine what a fully concerted set of memes being run by your biological hardware could do – in later chapters we will look at the subject of memes and their effect on biological and biophysical systems.

Psiops management applications

The most enduring feature of the economy is its cyclic nature. Booms and slumps follow each other like the seasons. Many suggestions have been made about why this should be so, but these are of no concern to us here. The point is that we have to accept the trade cycle as a permanent feature of the economic climate. It is necessary to be prepared for its vagaries. Boom times are seemingly easy to cope with. Optimism rules. But this gives rise to a dangerous sense of complacency, when nearly everyone forgets that all booms eventually come to an end. Managers think that the growth will go on forever and make their plans accordingly. When the inevitable recession arrives, they discover that they have over-extended themselves, having invested in property and plant which cannot be employed at full capacity when markets contract. Small businesses go under, whilst the large ones find their profits vanishing.

Seasons of recession bring their obvious difficulties. Markets shrink, profitability falls and unit production costs rise. Public sector bodies are equally at the mercy of economic cycles. When funds were plentiful, additional staff were engaged and activities were undertaken which, when the squeeze came, proved to be dispensable. And in difficult times, demoralisation set in and essential services had to be withdrawn. The use of remote viewing enables the manager to psychically spy on the global decision makers in the banking world who set interest rates and forewarns the psiops manager as to future trading conditions. Even in the worst of times – such as the current 'war on terror' – there are micro-climates of opportunity (MCOs), which offer companies the chance to make money and enable public sector organisations to provide as good a service as possible using the resources available. To find these areas of opportunity and to take advantage of them, four things are needed:

• Psiops managers must preserve a positive outlook, and use RV and RS to recognise opportunities even in the face of shrinking markets and economic gloom. Recessions provide the chance to consolidate, optimise and sow the seeds of success when the next boom comes, for when it does, every effort must be devoted to making the most of it.

- Reaction times of companies and organisations must be short (a matter of months), to enable them to take advantage of the opportunities as they arise. Using RS to scan the minds of the key players that affect one's business gives the psiops manager the opportunity to react to change in real-time.

- Organisations must be adaptable and reactive – 'light on their feet'. To this end, the use of remote sensing by managers to scan for bottlenecks in their own business and the suppliers they depend on enables a faster response to change.

- The ability to remotely view and sense all aspects upon which one's business depends can mean the difference between bankruptcy and success. The simple remote sensing protocols in this chapter provide the basis upon which the more sophisticated remote sensing and remote viewing techniques depend.

FOUR

DIRECTED ATTENTION

Directed attention (DA) is a tool to increase efficiency of mind and body, and these DA exercises follow on from the exercises given in the previous chapters:

1. Focus your mind on your body and relax all muscles from toes to head.

2. Direct your attention to the memory of a positive emotion-laden scene such as an old love affair. Then, direct your attention onto your mind's eye. Return to the memory: this induces positive hormones and neu- roelectrical stimuli that calm the brain stress system. The mind is connected to the body by the nervous system which has nerve endings that produce neu- ropeptides transferred to every part of body by monocytes.

The state of mind is mirrored in every part of the body, especially the immune system.

---

3. Practise the remote sensing of a person you know. The positive bodily state you induced preceding RS will now be automatically equated by your brain as being the

result of RS. This causes a positive feedback loop to occur which boosts your RS potential.

Practise directed attention

As described previously, one can use directed attention to break chaotic feedback loops. By fixating on a positive memory, symbol or phrase, then practising RS, the positive bodily reaction is associated with RS. By using directed attention in this way, you enter a new mental feedback loop that is based on the practice of RS. Directed attention is defined by a state of awareness where the focus of attention is coherent and concentrated on one spot, rather like a laser.

Directed attention is the prime tool for switching off the brain stress system, to initiate the theta states of consciousness. Bringing the mind–body interface into synchronicity (stress control, curing psychosomatic disease), we use attention directed on the *locus coeruleus*: stress destroys efficiency, clear minds enhance efficiency.

To this end the first and most important use of directed attention is to visualise the *locus coeruleus* part of the brain. Dr Carl Simonton found he could extend the lifespan of terminally ill cancer patients by getting them to visualise their immune systems and to imagine the white corpuscles therein gobbling up cancer cells. Similarly, a remote sensing expert can use this methodology to relax. There are a series of biophysical techniques to augment the one already described in this chapter. Together these methods supplant biofeedback using a computer electroencephalophograph (EEG) monitor and video display unit (VDU), as used by the military in the past, and with neural implants at present.

1. Visualise yourself inside the *locus coeruleus*.

2. Once you have directed attention inside your brain, command the *locus coeruleus* to ignore everything which is not life-threatening and has no bearing on your goals.

3. Visualise all your goals as if you had completed them. Do this in chronological order starting with your life goal(s) and finishing with goals you need for the present. Add the caveat that every time you are in this state you can upgrade your goals as you learn and experience more.

4. Feel the positive neurochemical state achieved by bringing the reptilian brain into synchrony with the rest of the brain stress system.

5 Command yourself to feel this way every time you do something to achieve your goals and/or practise RS.

As you can see, we are using positive feedback to help you achieve your goals and/or use RS, so you won't find them difficult but instead you'll feel invigorated.

Below are a few further techniques to help facilitate directed attention:

1. Diaphragm breathing. Breathe in through the nose; your diaphragm drops and stomach rises; breathe out through the nose; your diaphragm rises and stomach drops. This increases lung capacity, lowers heart rate and stimulates nerve endings in the nose which are

connected to the brain. This exercise links your brain's attention with that of your body, something we have learnt to ignore as we grow older.

2. Practise directed attention on one specific RS of a person you know, while listening to baroque music in a relaxed atmosphere. This stimulates alpha rhythms in the brain, increasing learning potential and memory. It then connects directed attention with this feeling of relaxation, so your body craves the relaxing feel of directed attention which has been connected with the relaxed state. By this method of positive feedback, directed attention is rapidly inculcated.

You can also practise concentrating your directed attention on your pulse or you can use a heart monitor to fix your attention on your heart beat. By fixing directed attention, you can learn to lower your heartbeat at will, again linking directed attention with the relaxed state of being. This exercise inculcates deep alpha states (see table, page 38). Slow pulse or heartbeats (originally heard in your mother's womb) have a profound effect on internal state, automatically lowering brainwave rhythms. Conversely, loud, chaotic sounds have a negative and destabilising effect on one's mind.

Orderly, peaceful environments stimulate orderly, effective remote sensing.

Using directed attention
Once you have practised the exercises above a little, fixate directed attention on your brain. Concentrate all your directed attention on the thalamus, this being part of the limbic

system of your brain associated with attention. The thalamus is the organ of attention in the brain. The brain can be divided into three domains. The most primitive area is clustered around the spinal cord and is called the brain stem, or the reptilian hindbrain. Around this is the limbic system. This part of the brain is associated with emotion, memory and most importantly attention, which is linked with the thalamus. By fixating your directed attention on your thalamus, you can reprogramme this part of the brain to alter your attention span and the quality thereof. Modern living and TV have caused a diminution in our attention to the level where we can only digest 20-second soundbites. To progress in RS, one must be able to fixate one's attention on the target person, and improve the quality of one's attention until it reaches directed attention.

This in fact means you are learning how to raise your biophysical fields from morphogenetic latency to primary consciousness, wherein they can leave the body and remotely view distant sites. To do this, the quality of your attention must be raised. By using what is called the Simonton Method of Psychoneural Interaction on your thalamus, you can reprogram your brain to elevate your attention to directed attention.

This is analogous to changing a torch beam into a laser beam. Visualise yourself inside the thalamus. Get a mental broom out and metaphorically clean out all blockages and data filters in the organ of attention. Command the thalamus to let all sensory data through. Go systematically through all six senses (remote sensing/extra-sensory perception being the sixth) and clean all the data channels. See your attention as a bright star epicentred in your thalamus (the epicentre of attention). Command the epicentre of attention to shine a bright white light of perception into the thalamus that becomes coherent and focuses down into the mental laser light of directed attention. Command this mental laser to illuminate your entire thalamus and command your attention to focus as directed attention on RS. Command your thalamus to give you an unlimited attention span, to eliminate all negative programmes that disrupt your attention. To engage all unused neurones and neuronal networks to boost your attention to directed attention. Then to elevate this directed attention to fixate on RS data being received by your biophysical vehicle as you scan another person.

You can then visualise your directed attention travelling from your thalamus through a mental screen, which is the doorway into the biophysical vehicle, to raise its consciousness from latent morphogenetic functioning to primary consciousness, where your biophysical vehicle is aware of the outside world.

Next practise your RS from this state of consciousness. With practise, every time you engage directed attention, your brain and biophysical fields will automatically engage this programme. By positive feedback, the practice of directed attention-enhanced biophysical RS will make you more and more efficient at RS: one can use directed attention to break chaotic feedback loops by fixating on a positive memory, symbol or phrase.

Use the mental laser light of directed attention as the cursor in the biophysical cyberspace of your paranormal world. This technique can be used to rewrite the memes hardwired into your neural net (see Chapter Six) and/or one can use DA to enter a new mental feedback loop using visualisation on RV scenes.

What really happens

The following table compares the four main types of brain rhythm and their relationship to psi:

>14 cycles per second	Beta rhythm	Stressed consciousness
7–14 cycles per second	Alpha rhythm	Unstressed consciousness, daydreaming. This is the most efficient waking state. Lower levels are the doorway to the subconscious and can be induced by using DA.
4–7 cycles per second	Theta rhythm	Dreaming state; interface with delta-doorway to the unconscious. This can be induced by DA and augmented by brain stress system modification.
<4 cycles per second	Delta rhythm	Dead to the world in deep, dreamless sleep. This state is open to experienced RS operators, and is the gateway to psychotronic realms unknown in the West.

Applications of directed attention
Problem solving:

1. Gather as much information as possible.

2. Feed it into your subconscious via DA in the alpha state.

3. Forget the problem and come back to it later using DA.

4. The solution will come (back) to you in a spark of inspiration.

5. Develop the idea while using RS to optimise it, then focus your DA on the prefrontal lobes of the brain, where higher cognitive activity takes place to fully develop the data into a workable mental model and solution to the problem with that person. We only use a tiny proportion of our brain power; estimates range from less than 10 per cent to 0.2 per cent (the latter figure is Einstein's). We can use DA to open up our brain function to higher operancy – these higher levels of cognitive function enable a quantum leap in business functioning. A practical example is the discovery of benzene by Kekule. He dreamt of a snake biting its own tail and made a jump of awareness from chain to ring structure. Another is Archimedes coming up with the idea to test whether the king's crown was made out of gold or not while daydreaming in the bath.

Wasted time on trains, stations and airports and slack periods in offices can be used for DA with eyes open, as can 'active breaks' on the golf course or squash court during the day to recharge one's batteries. This is useful for breaking negative mental feedback loops that one has become fixated on and drain one's energy.

We learn to fixate our attention on things other people want us to be aware of – we can learn to centre our attention on things of our choosing, in the process seeing things as they are and becoming fitter, more energetic and efficient in the process. A remote sensing adept chooses his own goals within the constraints laid down by her or himself and prevailing world conditions.

Remote sensing

Following instructions in the example above, substitute a person for the problem – view the person and RS a way to deal with them instead of a problem.

Psiops applications: microclimates of opportunity – the organisation in a changing world

Come what may, every organisation must satisfy the desires of its customers or clients. People must continue to want the organisation's products and purchase them in the future. Strategic planning should be geared, above all, to this end. Planning ahead is, however, bedevilled by insuperable problems. The world is changing so quickly that normal forecasting has become impossible. There are too many imponderables and the relation between causes and effects is poorly understood.

Nowhere can this be seen more clearly than in the world of business. Economics is looked upon as a science, but economists readily admit that their discipline is in a stage comparable to that of science before Newton. Its assertions are effectively untested, since they are based on information of poor quality which is difficult to evaluate. In global and national economies, no-one knows what are symptoms and what are causes.

Remote viewing, on the other hand, was developed by the military to enable psi-warfare operators to look into the future. It therefore enables the psiops–capable company to accurately map the probability of future events. (For a fuller account of the history and uses of remote viewing, please consult my previous book, *Remote Viewing*.)

Almost certainly, important factors are not being taken

into account by psi-blind companies. Trends are easily explained – with hindsight. And the impressive mathematical models upon which economic forecasting depends rest ultimately on nothing more substantial than beliefs. In such a situation it is essential never to take any action whose success depends upon the accuracy of a forecast. Only remote viewing enables the company and it management to look into the future.

The only alternative for non psiops-capable companies is to make the best of what comes along, using short-term forecasting aimed at achievable goals. Psiops-capable companies can accurately foresee events a short time in the future using remote viewing. This is the basic principle of psiops management. As part of this strategy, it is necessary to seek out those microclimates of opportunity (MCOs) which exist even in the worst of times. These are corners of the economy, often quite specialised, where the demand for products and services continues and possibly even grows. During recessions, accountants specialising in company liquidations thrive! But whatever the activity in which the organisation is engaged, MCOs can be found. The difficulty for the company is to accept that strategic planning must direct its attention not only to long-term projects, but also to hunting out and grasping these opportunities, which may appear unglamorous but could turn out to be lifelines; the first company to seize such initiatives has the advantage and is in a position to become a market leader. Remote viewing enables a company to see these opportunities.

The first step in psiops management is to become remote viewing capable and to use this ability in a goal-directed respect focused on the fundamental principle – that the company exists to satisfy its clients. This applies to the organisation, its culture and everyone associated with it in any way.

How to find microclimates of opportunity

The first stage in finding microclimates of opportunity is to shortlist the possibilities. Then use remote viewing and sensing, to firm out the microclimate of opportunity.

The systematic approach uses remote viewing and sensing to:

1. Determine the key decisions which have to be made and how the core competencies of the company can be utilised in new ways to service customers' needs. To this end, think:
   a) Customer driven: what can the company do to satisfy customers' wants better?
   b) Service driven: what services can the company provide to satisfy customers' needs better?
   c) Commitment to excellence: what improvements can be made in the ways that things are done in the company? How these might be utilised in new and profitable ways?

   Look at remote viewing scenarios of the future where you make systematic changes to the business in accord with the above principles – which changes work?

2. Decide what can be done to optimise the long-term prospects of the organisation from the information revealed by the above questions. Use remote viewing and sensing in combination with directed attention to examine these questions and their answers; then consider the possible future outcomes.

Remote viewing and sensing may reveal possible microclimates of opportunity which could exist for the company, so look at possible futures where you start producing new products and services.

On average, psiops companies will have a couple of years' forecasting advantage over their competitors, and thus be in a favourable position to take advantage of MCOs. This lead, in conjunction with the positive feedback which is part of the process, will allow the company to occupy the niche created by the MCO, allowing it to become market leader in this sector. In this case remote viewing and sensing is vital as it allows the psiops manager to psychically scan competitors and to look for favourable trading conditions and milieus.

Competitors, on the other hand, will find themselves blind to future events, thus they will be permanently trying to catch up whilst the remote-viewing-capable rival is drawing ahead; month by month the gap will widen, as a benign cycle sets in. This not only gives the advantage to the first company taking advantage of the MCO; that advantage increases as time goes on. Eventually, the remote viewing/sensing-able companies gain such a lead over competitors that their rivals have to drop out of the sector entirely as they will find it impossible to make a profit. Precisely the same principles apply in the public sector, exposed as it now is to commercial forces. Thus we come to important lessons of psiops management:

1. The first company in the field has the advantage over competitors. Thus the reason for the importance of remote viewing and sensing.

2. Positive feedback – the law of increasing returns – applies; most MCOs are likely to be in high-tech fields and a position, once secured, can be strengthened as time goes on.

3. Having a couple of years' lead over competitors means that a psiops-capable company can build up an unassailable advantage, as positive feedback means that the edge over competitors is constantly increasing.

FIVE

THE GEOGRAPHY OF ATTENTION AND THE PRINCIPLES OF SUCCESS

The geography of attention can be categorised as:

1. Conscious: the compartmentalised separated, so-called 'normal' attention.

2. Subconscious: the hidden area of consciousness that directs our attention, moods and emotions.

3. Unconscious: the 'empty' void from which the intelligence that directs our bodies (morphogenetic fields) and from which creative ideas derive.

4. Collective Unconscious (term coined by Jung): the group attention of man which is the repository of the collective memory and from which we can access everything that is known by our competitors. This is the biophysical domain talked about by Jung when he described archetypes residing in a universal sea of consciousness.

Mapping mindsets
Use your newfound power of DA to explore these areas in another person. Use the start-up procedure from Chapter

Four to enter DA, then RS the person of interest, system-atically mapping out the conscious parts of their mind. Next map out their subconscious, keeping a log of your findings and how they fit in with your image of that person and their mindset. Next, use directed attention fixated on their unconscious to map out the totality of their mindset, keeping a log of your findings. Finally, use RS to journey into the collective unconscious to view how that person is connected to that mega-thoughtform. Take special interest in any archetypes – the seminal memes that define specific behaviour, such as hero, king or fool – and denizens of the sea of universal conscious-ness that are linked to that person. Keep focused on your RS of the person's links with the universal unconscious's geography and inhabitants, as if from a distance. Do not channel or contact any of the inhabitants.

This practice raises the morphogentic biophysical fields to primary consciousness and begins to raise them from there to high-order consciousness, where they can think for themselves independently of the brain.

Mapping the mental pathways of the person

Pathways of attention can be traced using the following ideas. The creative part of the mind is in the unconscious which has links with the collective unconscious. This is reached via the remote viewer's subconscious which is accessible during dreaming, daydreaming and DA. RS allows the experienced operator to access all areas of the geography of attention. This means that RS operators can affect their own bodies and those of other people by using the unconscious and group unconscious respectively.

Try to remotely sense the person during the day using

the protocols in this book. Then try at night while they are asleep. Notice that the information you get from them while they are asleep naturally mirrors their underlying urges and needs. Take your time mapping out the fundamental drives that motivate that person. From there, let your biophysical vehicle be drawn into their unconscious so you can scan the foundations of their mindset. You can begin to see the bedrock of their psyche and appreciate the early conditioning that moulded the way their mindset conformed to pre-existing areas in the unconscious.

Let your RS then drift down to see the connections of that person with the universal unconscious. See their links with this sea of consciousness as cables.

Tap into each cable and note what idea sets are contained on this mental link. Scan the emotion stream and content of the mental stream. See which way it is flowing. Locate nodes of this mind stuff from the universal unconscious in the higher areas of the person's mindset and the networking of these nodes of mind stuff, which underpins their mind.

Finally, follow the mental links to the archetypes and other power sources in the universal unconscious to appreciate the true forces behind the person you are scanning. This methodology can be developed in paranormal-psychoneural ways to treat mental problems.

Try the following exercises:

- Simulate business contacts, interviews and sales strategies with people. Use DA to remotely sense the people in the forthcoming situation. RS the people to see what is the best approach with them to obtain the optimum successful outcome. Then RS to reach the actual event and analyse what is happening in the people at that time. Compare this with your initial RS to optimise it. Use remote sensing to change your response to that forth-coming situation until it suits your requirements.

The act of RS and mental simulation of people's reactions (cognitive RS interaction) optimises your response to people and ups the probability of the future going as you wish.

- Take five-minute breaks during which you direct your attention to a RS of a person you wish to interact with. Amplify RS by using negative entropy from the environment to boost your awareness. This negative entropy is the life-force in the countryside. RS the person while linking with energy from the countryside will naturally attune your biophysical RS vehicle to that person. Because you are boosting your biophysical field with this energy, RS is amplified. It also means that your scanning of that person will make them feel better. This adaptive energy – negative entropy or life-force – also boosts your RS so you can scan any person of interest.

Feedback loops of people's attention take up more and more of their energy throughout the day. These feedback loops are broken by sleep or by directed attention on a new cycle of attention (partially done while relaxing or having a gin and tonic!) Practising RS is the perfect way to tap into these negative feedback loops in other people and find out what motivates their behaviour. This enables the RS oper-ator to realise how the mindset of that person is controlled by these attention loops. This enables strategies to be developed in working with that person which tap into their natural programming. Biophysical energy, which can be used in RS by tapping into adaptive energy locals, boosts RS, so these phenomena can be seen clearly.

- Exercises carried out only as a mental simulation in the mind have a similar effect as real exercise on the body. One can use five minute breaks to improve golf swing, squash stroke or tennis serve; this also makes one feel more energetic because it interrupts depleting cycles of attention we can easily slip in to. Remote viewing of a golf course and a subsequent round of golf is a good way to develop one's RV/RS awareness.

- Use five-minute breaks to actuate DA, and thereby activate biophysical RS awareness. Once in this state, let your RS attention go where it wants. This method allows you to focus on unconscious intents you are not aware of and opportunities you may not have foreseen, by letting yourself home in on people of interest to your subconscious.

A knock-on effect of this exercise is integrating your subconscious and unconscious mind with your conscious mind. This process is intimately linked with the biophysical vehicle's elevation from simple morphogenetic functioning to high-order consciousness.

Remote sensing and self-image

One's RS attention is intimately related to one's self-image (supraprogramme of individual) and the programmes we have acquired since birth. The Supraprogramme is built from mental programmes and based on mental algorithms – the way data is processed, normally in a linear fashion but it can be in a lateral or holistic manner, analogous to linear and parallel processing. Try these methods of RS training:

- Fix your directed attention on RS and empower it with negative entropy from power sources such as the countryside or power spots such as Stonehenge. By remotely sensing different locations, imagine your RS biophysical vehicle picking up adaptive energy from its surroundings to 'flesh out' the biophysical body. From RS, one can begin to change oneself and others by reprogramming the supraprogramme, mental programmes and optimising algorithms. This remote sensing of the operator frees up biophysical energy and enhances brain function, so the operator can make use of her or his biophysical field which is giving them data.

   This idea can be developed in the RS milieu to home in on people's energy fields. Young people have generally got larger, more powerful energy bodies unless they are infants. This surplus of energy can be used for telekinesis – such as poltergeist activity seen in pubescent females. People who have had children will be seen to have lost adaptive energy from their biophysical fields – holes may be apparent in their energy bodies. Negative people will be seen to have dark fields around their energy bodies as they are linked with negative archetypes from the universal unconscious. RS operators will have large fields which may shine like they have an inner power source. RS people you know as well as celebrities, log your results and begin to build up a morphology of the biophysical forms present.

- RS a person you are going to meet and send them negative entropy, adaptive energypositive emotional stimuli. This leads on to remote influencing (see glossary). One can always do business with people as long as you contact their true being with right intent. Convince that person that there is something in it for them – your consciousness is connected to theirs. So if one simulates this meeting of minds to the point where you felt it had been a success, the actual meeting will be influenced to such an extent that it will invariably go to a positive outcome.

- DA fixed on RS of people you are going to meet in the future allows you to optimise your business as well as your social life. Time management – fitting everything needful into one's life by fast-time RS of the people one is going to meet that day – is best done just before one gets up as you are naturally in the alpha state and in direct contact with your subconscious, so throughout the day your subconscious will subtly compel you to follow this path. This technique will make you aware that we are all affected by negative programmes in our subconscious, that have made us do, and follow, things that led to disaster, delays and stress (see RS of the future in Chapter Nine).

We all live in our 'heads', so use RS of future meetings with people to become aware of negative and positive feedback from the 'experiment of life'. Evaluate courses of action so one can become a goal-orientated leader. Exercise one's brain and RS awareness like one's muscles.

We learn to fixate our attention on things other people want us to be aware of. We can learn to centre our attention on things of our own choosing, in the process seeing things as they are and becoming fitter, more energetic and efficient. The psiops adept choose their own goals within the constraints laid down by themselves, the company and prevailing world conditions. By this method one can scan what is going on in people's heads and learn how to see the lies and traps people lay for the unwary. RS is superbly useful for finding leaks in organisations and people who are betraying you.

When remote sensing people, those who are untrustworthy will have a black energy field. Intelligence agents in the Western Milieu have a biophysical field that appers to the RS adept as a reptile-looking energy body as all their actions are controlled by the reptilian complex in their brain. This imprints the image on their morphogenetic field, as all their higher-level consciousness has been subsumed by the reptilian elements of dominance, submission and enforcing the status quo. They are essentially devolved awareness that appears human but is in fact a low level, obedience-trained automaton.

Psiops applications: the human factor

So far, we have not mentioned much about human factors such as the personal development of staff. But if an organisation's plans are to be fully effective and brought to fruition, planning cannot be considered apart from the personal plans and goals of the people involved. Failure to appreciate this is one of the reasons why management initiatives encounter resistance within the organisation. It is for this reason empathic awareness is so valuable to managers as it allows them to intuit what staff are really thinking and feeling about new initiatives.

It may come as a surprise to learn that some of the factors

that bring about this resistance are a consequence of human biology. This will be discussed shortly; for the present, it is necessary only to consider the effects – inertia and resistance to change. When the world is changing all around, the result is disintegration, decline and loss of market share and profitability.

This brings us to the first rule of psiops management:

Take account of human performance and aspirations

Like the crew and passengers in a boat, everyone in an organisation has a stake in its success. Both managers and managed must share the same goals. There is no conflict of interest. A successful company allows managers and staff to develop their own goals, and in doing so, the organisation does likewise. RS enables one to monitor this process. This brings us to the second rule of psiops management:

Psiops begins with training – fostering positive attitudes

Training is the starting point for the implementation of psiops management. The first step is to build positive 'internal models'. We all carry in our heads a personal picture of the world. It is a product of our traditions, training, customs and prejudices. This is our 'internal model'. When the reality of life and the actions of those around us conform to the model, we feel secure and relaxed. When they do not conform, we feel disturbed. This can be looked at in another way. Perhaps, in truth, what disturbs us is not events or the actions of other people, but the model that we carry around with us. At best, our model bears only a passing resemblance to the world; we do, indeed, 'see through a glass darkly', since our picture is a product of our life's experience. Once this is realised, there is no need to feel disturbed. Unfortunately, so tightly are we chained to our internal models that this advice is easier to give than take! Use remote sensing to psychically study your mind and the group mind of the company to see what I mean.

- Establish the goal by remote viewing the future to see what works. Everything else but the goal should be regarded as an encumbrance and dropped. This is essentially the responsibility of the leaders within an organisation, since it is they who establish its culture. Leaders must promulgate goal-orientated action and ignore petty distractions and sources of annoyance that do not fit in with corporate and personal goals.

- Individuals must become aware of microclimates of opportunity within their sphere of responsibility and actively seek them out using RV and RS.

- Everyone must develop the practice of continuously revising their internal models by internal RS to make their goals easier to achieve. If it works, do it again; if not, find out why.

- Discard all ideas and attitudes that do not help in achieving goals, use RV to see the effect of each change in ideas and attitudes on the fulfilment of the goal.

- Establish a psiops infrastructure within the organisation, which nurtures and propagates positive internal models such as RV and RS. Maintain a focus on one, all-important rule: the organisation exists to satisfy its clients.

What are those to do who find themselves in lowly positions in organisations permeated by negative attitudes? The difficulty is that the culture can only be changed from the top downwards, and even then, as we have seen, inertia hinders desirable change. For anyone in such circumstances, the best advice is to move on, resolving to discover more about any potential employer in the future. But moving on is not always a practicable possibility. What then? There is nothing to stop anyone with only limited influence from developing positive attitudes. Even in a demoralised organisation, there is no excuse for forgetting that customers and clients come first.

Paradoxically, circumstances such as these offer particularly fertile ground for finding microclimates of opportunity (MCOs) using RV and RS, and it is quite possible to establish islands of high morale. Seeding the company with positive memes can dramatically change the company culture. The alternative is to grumble about management and speculate about what will happen at the next round of reorganisation. This is debilitating and makes the work harder. By being adept at RS one can find out what is really going on in the head of the person who runs the company and become indispensable by learning to empathise with him or her as well as having psiops skills.

Act first think later

The theorists would have us believe that business decisions are all made on the basis of full knowledge and a rational weighing-up of all the relevant factors. Consumers, producers, banks and every other agent in the economy is infinitely smart. Thus, if two businessmen or managers or staff sit down to negotiate a deal or discuss tactics, the theory assumes that each can instantly foresee every possible outcome of each of the alternative possible courses of action, and so choose the best. Everyone knows that the real world is not like this, but the theory has not caught up. It is astonishing that this ivory-tower view has ever been accepted. Neither economies nor organisations act in a perfectly rational way. But from the economists' point of view, the notion that economic systems are the product of perfectly rational decisions is very useful, because it makes the economy amenable to the kind of analysis which is their professional stock in trade, and so it keeps them in business. Humans, the cogs in this economic machine, do not act as perfectly rational entities. Humans have intentions and emotions, act in deliberate ways and make decisions according to agendas of their own, in the light of their personal outlook. Taken together, all these factors mean that in practice, humans are less than perfectly smart. We make our decisions according to our feelings – and rationalise afterwards. It is for this reason RS is so vital to running a good business.

The state of affairs described above might be termed 'pseudo-rationality' – there is an illusion of rational decision making. This 'rationality deficit' seems to have a biological origin, arising from the capricious workings of the limbic system, the emotional part of the brain; the part that really drives us and determines how we view the world, what attracts our attention, what we remember, what we forget and what decisions we make. We have all been involved in business transactions whose outcome has been influenced by personal feelings rather than the merits of the subject of the negotiations. This is an example of the mischief that can be worked by the limbic system. A good remote sensor learns this and uses it to her/his advantage on all occasions.

Because rational decision making is an illusion, one aspect of psiops management is concerned with considering the limbic system and seeking ways to bring it under control. This was why we discussed the brain stress system at length.

In psiops management we must achieve the following:

1. Align emotions with goals by RS.

2. Think tidily by remote sensing one's own thought processes.

3. Increase the power of memory by using autovisualisation on the hypothalamus. Inputting images directly into this brain centre by internal RS develops the memory palace (see page 68).

4. Increase the power of attention by focussing RS on the thalamus and then looking at the object of attention.

5. Increase the manager's ability to cope with information by operating in theta.

6. Promote positive feedback when staff implement management initiatives by making them feel positive; one knows by RS just the right thing to say to them.

7. Understand how important the 'feelgood' factor is.

The above goals are all achieved by lowering the brain stress system arousal level.

Axioms of psiops management

Consideration of the causes of pseudo rationality leads us to the axioms of psiops management:

1. Pseudo rationality in staff and managers is the root cause of inertia and resistance of the organisation to change.

2. The rationality deficit can be minimised by remote viewing and sensing so that decisions approach the 'perfectly smart' limit.

3. Negative feedback in companies and institutions causes resistance to change. In the worst cases, not only does little come of attempts to initiate change, but the organisation becomes more and more resistant, as the number of failed attempts increases.

4. Positive feedback to promote desirable change can be promoted by working at the level of people's feelings. This applies not only to individuals, but at a company level, where it can optimise the 'corporate rationality' of the company culture. Memes developed by the author and given in later chapters can repattern the company for optimum performance.

5. Remote viewing should be used to see the future. Do not imagine that you know what the future will be like without first looking. See Chapter Nine for more information.

We now look at how remote sensing can be developed to understand the dynamics of failure.

The destructive feedback cycle

The principles that apply are based on remote sensing technology:

1. All information has to be processed through the brain. New data is not dealt with in isolation, but integrated with old material of a similar nature.

2. Emotional content (feelings which arise during the training) is also woven into the memory of the data and linked to similar feelings experienced in the past.

When learning new ways of working, you will link these in your mind with any previous attempts to change your habits. Most of these previous attempts will have caused you stress. Whenever similar new material is presented in similar circumstances, it will connect with that memory and the stress will spring back into life just as if a playback button was being pressed. And it is not only stress which is recorded in this way, only waiting for the press of the playback button – a whole collection of similar negative feelings are lurking beneath the surface, originating in stressful experiences, some from long ago in childhood. As a result, when attempts are made to implement new management material, there is resistance. This bad feeling is felt as stress whenever any attempt is made to implement the new management material. People feel ill-at-ease with it. A real effort of will is required to carry it through to completion and which can be exhausting. The person or workforce will try to reduce this stress by implementing the new material slowly or finding excuses not to carry it out.

To make matters worse, managers and staff are liable to strike attitudes and fail to talk to each other. The workforce can lose confidence with its managers and might not see the use of the changes. Since new practices cause stress at the best of times, if subordinates lack confidence in their managers, they will, at best, go through the motions of change, with no real commitment. The end result is an organisation stuck in a rut, unable to change.

There are two factors at the core of the destructive feedback cycle problem:

1. The long-term future is unpredictable. As was discussed, organisations take on average three years to implement significant changes. This places an impossible strain on the leadership, since it is impossible to make reliable forecasts about markets and the trading environment three years ahead. It is certain that top management will make mistakes, which will be noticed and remembered by the workforce, causing erosion of confidence in the leadership. The longer this goes on, the worse it becomes, frustrating any attempt to change company culture. Thus, poor planning shows the workforce that there is no real need for new working practices because 'they don't know what they're doing anyway'. But if the reaction time of the organisation could be reduced to just a few months, then the leadership need look only that far into the future. In a fast-changing, chaotic world, tactical plans looking mainly to the short-term future will be a lot nearer to the mark than any long-term strategic plan. With reliable tactical planning, the workforce has more faith in its leaders and is therefore willing to put itself out to carry out their initiatives.

More importantly, RV a few months into the future requires less energy than far future RV.

2. We make our decisions according to our feelings, and rationalise later – do it first, think afterwards. Psiops expunges the destructive feedback cycle and enables effective management. This is done by altering the brain stress system's functioning, so that it operates in a more relaxed state, and using RS in one's business dealings.

Why things can turn sour

What makes people so reluctant to change? Perhaps the most important reason is the way the human brain is put together. Animal brains are made up of a series of layers. The brains of humans and the higher mammals have three layers, with the reptilian complex at the core. In birds and the lower mammals, there is no cortex and the limbic system forms the outer layer. Reptiles possess only the reptilian complex. The reptilian complex, as mentioned before, is concerned with stress. The reassurance of familiar situations and knowing one's place in the pecking order puts the reptilian complex into a settled state. Lack of confidence stimulates the reptilian complex, causing anxiety and stress. Once this is appreciated, it is not difficult to understand why sound tactical planning is so important; faith in the leadership reassures and so permits workers to get on with their jobs, free from nagging fears and doubts. This brings us to the third rule of psiops management:

Leaders should do everything in their power to inspire confidence, as this makes staff more willing to follow their leader's wishes

---

Poorly defined pecking order is something that can acti-vate the reptilian complex. Some management theories have advocated putting managers and the rest of the work-force on an equal footing. There is nothing wrong with this, but it is the manager's responsibility to manage. If staff do not know where they stand, they feel insecure. To prevent this, managers should make their subordinates feel valued.

This gives us the fourth rule of psiops management:

***

Managers give those around them a sense of worth to enable them to influence their superiors, and to get their staff to follow them

***

This is done by keeping the reptilian part of the brain happy. Anything which elevates the individual's sense of self-importance will reassure the reptilian complex, reduc-ing anxiety and engendering feelings of security and well-being. If you promote another person's sense of worth as you talk to them, your views will be associated with a positive feeling. Every time they remember what you said to them, they will re-live this pleasing state which you sparked off. Positive feelings will occur when your superi-ors think about your views; likewise, your staff will be more willing to do what you want.

How we feel affects how well we can reason and think. If we are anxious and tense, we just can't think properly.

Making our feelings work for us

Although we imagine that we make our decisions rationally, recent research suggests that it isn't like this at all. Confronted with a mass of data, the brain somehow sums up the total situation and makes our decisions for us on the basis of our feelings. According to the theory, this happens in the limbic system. When we come to action, the cortex, which is the seat of logical reasoning, apparently plays second fiddle to this emotional core.

Depending on our emotional state, the cortex can be quiet or busy. But if it is busy, we cannot easily take note of and assimilate what is going on around us. We become inattentive, may not hear all that people say, find it hard to concentrate and may have difficulty in remembering things.

This gives us the fifth rule of psiops management:

A relaxed state of mind is more attentive, can store more data and retrieve more data than an anxious one

This is a familiar experience; we excuse our lack of attention by saying that 'we were distracted'. The point is that the poor attention is related to our emotional state. The emotional overtones associated with anything we remember or learn are at least as important as the knowledge itself. If we didn't like a teacher, we probably didn't like the subject and, years later, that subject can still bring back bad feelings. And of course, the converse is equally true. Remembering something that we learnt whilst in a good frame of mind also recalls those good feelings and this drives us to strive further in that direction. Thus, management material imparted to staff in a relaxed frame of mind is not only absorbed more effectively; when the time comes to remember and apply what was taught, the good feelings result in a motivation to act upon it. The ramifications of this process do not stop here. The state of the limbic system also affects our general level of stress, by influencing the action of various hormone-producing glands. One effect is to simulate a 'fight-or-flight' response in the body.

If managers and staff are stressed at work, their bodies are filled with hormones that are telling their bodies to fight or flee. This is exactly what you would need if you had just seen a sabre-toothed tiger coming in your direction. It is less useful in an office or factory. We get used to this state, but it is exhausting. It causes, amongst other things:

- Susceptibility to disease.

- Reduction in efficiency due to tiredness. Many people are almost permanently in this state.

- Actual illness: in the US, tens of billions of dollars are lost annually due to absenteeism caused by stress-related disease.

It can be seen that a reduction in stress would greatly reduce disease and absenteeism. Finally, there is one further aspect of stress to be considered. The reptilian complex is preoccupied with urges like hunger, sex and place in the pecking order. When it gets hold of an idea, it doesn't let go. This has important implications:

- At work, any disputes about dominance lead to a build-up of stress.

- Any change or threat to the status quo will cause stress. Examples include new working practices, new technology, reorganisation, as well as rumours of any of these. This is why changes should be presented as evolutionary,

so that staff will be able to pigeon-hole them into familiar categories.

• An organisation where people do not know exactly
   what they are doing and who they are doing it for will
   also breed stress. This is because the reptilian brain
   complex likes an ordered world and ritualistic activity,
   where it knows what is going on and feels secure.

This gives us the next three rules of psiops management:

Have clearly defined pecking orders. The ideal state is
hierarchical with a free flow of feedback

Introduce all new ideas as a continuation of what
people are doing already, not as something radically
new which will cause drastic changes and be
perceived as disruptive

Have an ordered business environment where working
practices are systematic, information is passed around in
an orderly way and there is an ethos where everyone
recognises that they are part of an organisation with a
sense of purpose – a psiops-trained organisation

This last point places particular responsibilities on psiops
managers, who must follow the rules just described to keep
their staff happy and contented. More importantly, they
should take advantage of another of the characteristics of the
reptilian complex – its goal-oriented nature. If a tethered

goat is placed in front of a crocodile, the reptile will ignore everything else and fix its attention on eating the goat. Similarly, psiops managers can learn to ignore the pettiness going on around and fixate on the goals. To do this, psiops managers must:

- Understand what is happening to themselves and their staff using RS.

- Define long, medium and short-term goals clearly, and optimise by using RV of the future.

- Assimilate these goals by internal RS so that they become the focus of the manager's actions as she or he carries out psiops.

Once the psiops manager has developed the habit of goal-direction, petty confrontations and irritations will be ignored. The activity of the brain stress system is thereby reduced. This increases general efficiency and the effectiveness of data acquisition, allowing the managers to achieve their goals more quickly and with less effort by use of RV and RS.

This gives us the ninth rule of psiops management:

Psiops managers are goal directed, and ignore whatever has no bearing on their goals

---

By these methods a benign cycle is set in train. Subordinates copy their managers' style, and this advantageous way of acting spreads throughout the organisation without the need for explicit instruction. People copy because the method brings results. You have boundless energy and your health has improved. In addition, you know how to motivate and lead people. You win their acceptance because you are not petty and ignore everything but the job at hand. Your subordinates feel comfortable and relaxed in your company. This positive meme is contagious. They are intrigued that you know something which they do not. Now is the right moment for explicit training in psiops management, when they, in turn, can repeat the process. Company culture is on the way to being transformed for the better, and the longer it continues, the more it improves.

Memory, habits and routines

The emotional core of the brain has a powerful influence on our activities. We discussed one aspect of memory; remembering things and how it is affected by emotion. When we feel relaxed and secure, we can remember whatever we have learnt more easily and accurately. But when we are agitated, it is difficult to think properly or bring to mind the things we need to remember. Psiops improves all aspects of the mind's functioning.

Another aspect of memory deals with skills; performing tasks such as swimming, driving and playing ball games. These can be improved by visualising yourself engaged in them; this is becoming an established practice amongst top athletes. Simulating an activity in your mind's eye, not only increases your skill at that task, but can also be used to practise and develop management skills, to the point that they become habitual. This is internal RS.

This leads to the tenth rule of psiops management:

Develop your memory and make the most of it

The memory can be developed by visualisation of the hypothalamus and internal RS of inputting information in an imaginative and imagery based style into this organ of the limbic system. Visualise within the hypothalamus a 'memory palace' with rooms filled with associated memories. In your memory palace, all work related information can be in one wing, with each room in that wing dedicated to subjects of your work. You then walk around this wing of the palace to recall information.

Habits and routines

Most of our activities are based on habits and routines. These are shaped by our view of the world. We slot ourselves into roles like actors in a play. But when we find ourselves in a role that we have not played before, we feel uneasy. The worst situation is the unexpected shock, which is less easily withstood than regular periodic shocks. Thus, when a company is failing, things are much more painful than regular reversals in a normal business scenario. Random shocks, for example, when jobs are chronically insecure, give rise to a state of 'free-floating anxiety'. Everyone affected is permanently on edge.

This can lead to depression, which can lead to irrational actions. This is not confined to individuals; it can affect companies, institutions and entire nations. An example of this on a national scale was the US post-9/11, when the country had been shaken by stock market collapse and business failures in all directions.

Free-floating anxiety leaves its scars even when conditions improve. The memory makes people ultra-cautious.

Customers may be well-off but unwilling to spend, and in an organisation, staff are unable and unwilling to change.

This gives us the eleventh rule of psiops management:

Free-floating anxiety caused by random shocks is a root cause of long-term problems in organisations

Free-floating anxiety should therefore be avoided at all costs. Give your staff the bad news regularly; never spring it on them at random or at an inopportune moment. Practice of remote sensing naturally cuts down on anxiety as it puts the brain stress system into a relaxed mode.

SIX

REMOTE SENSING AND UNKNOWN POTENTIALS

Unknown potentials are areas of awareness in the subconscious and unconscious that can be assimilated into one's consciousness. RS develops these whole areas of our being. This is the preface to a systematic study of biophysical fields. RS these unknown areas in others; the knock-on effect will be that you begin to see those unknown areas in yourself.

All we think we are is not all we are; in fact our subconscious and unconscious are only such because we do have not the appropriate tools to assimilate them into conscious awareness. Learning and using RS allows us to access all areas of our own awareness. Biophysical fields can be raised from morphogenetic latency to primary consciousness and beyond. Once this is done we can access information not normally available; for example past memories, all of which are stored in the brain like a hologram but are normally inaccessible. Use directed attention on RS attuned to an old memory in another person. See what you can make of their recall, then visualise what part of your brain you are drawn to in that person (it should be in the neocortex or hippocampus). Empower them with adaptive energy to open up this memory (negative entropy is an energy which rather than causing disorder brings order and consciousness into events as well as biophysical and physical being). Energy obtained from

RV of the countryside can empower the RS vehicle before this procedure. See if the memory clarifies. For memories you cannot access, fixate your attention on any memory in the person connected with the one you want to recall, then 'let go' and wait for the memory you want to appear in your own consciousness. If the memory is still not recalled, use directed attention to order their mind to find it and bring it to you. You may find that hours or days later, while you are in normal consciousness, it will surface in your own mind.

Relaxation programme

As a first exercise in stress management for RS performance, practise the following:

1. Lay down on a bed.

2. In your mind's eye, visualise your feet.

3. Imagine all the muscles in your feet becoming limp.

4. Visualise your ankles.

5. Imagine all the muscles in your ankles becoming limp.

6. Visualise your calves.

7. Imagine all the muscles in your calves becoming limp.

8. Visualise your knees and thighs.

9. Imagine all the muscles in your knees and thighs becoming limp.

10. Visualise your lower body.

11. Imagine all the muscles in your lower abdomen becoming limp.

12. Visualise your chest and back.

13. Imagine all the muscles in your chest and back becoming limp.

14. Visualise your arms.

15. Imagine all the muscles in your arms becoming limp.

16. Visualise your neck.

17. Imagine all the muscles in your neck becoming limp.

18. Visualise your head.

19. Imagine all the muscles in your head becoming limp.

20. Now imagine yourself floating to a grassy meadow.

21. Visualise the grass. Hear the birds sing. Feel the sun on your skin, the ground beneath your body. Smell the grass.

22. Visualise all your worries drifting from your body and evaporating in the sunlight.

23. Feel the sunlight filling your body with energy that

washes away the anxieties you have accumulated.

24. Tell yourself that you feel better than you have ever felt in your life.

25. Imagine your past experiences that caused your anxiety.

26. See the black vapour of these old anxieties being expelled from your body, to be replaced with positives habits.

27. Replace these old worries with the new, positive habits.

28. Choose one at a time for each day you practise and visualise these new habits easing out the old anxiety-inducing habits. These positive habits are called success software. They are the set of positive memes you will be introduced to in this book.

29. Next imagine your DA being fixated in your thalamus. Visualise a mental laser light expanding outward from your thalamus to encapsulate your whole brain, with the intent of total relaxation.

30. Visualise your DA reprogramming your brain to be in a theta state of relaxation whenever you practise RS.

31. Next practise RS of a site of interest. Link the feeling of relaxation with your RS practise, so every time you RS a site you naturally inculcate a relaxed state of mind in yourself. Thus by a process of positive feedback you get more relaxed every time you practise RS.

To implement this methodology:

1. Use the above relaxation programme to induce a theta state.

2. Fixate your awareness on the thalamus and focus the mental laser light of your DA on producing a mental screen in your mind's eye.

3. Visualise your biophysical body being made manifest in front of your mind's eye on the mental screen. Visualise the 'I' part of your attention – the epicentre of your DA – entering your biophysical RS vehicle.

4. Visualise your biophysical RS vehicle leaving your body and travelling to your workplace.

5. Allow your biophysical RS vehicle to scan all the personnel of interest and it will automatically sense what plans they have.

6. Next, RS future events connected with your career and business to see how these people influence your future.

7. RS a future where everything goes your way and begin to use RV to find how to get there from your present time-line.

Mind–brain modem
This, an interface between mind and body, is in the supplementary motor area (SMA), which lies in the top centre of the brain where the soft spot used to be. It excites as voluntary

acts in the brain pass to the body, and every time you decided to do something this area generates electrical activity.

The SMA was first discovered in the 1920s by the Canadian neurophysiologist Wilder Penfield as a side product of his search for the epileptic initiator in the brain. Neurophysiologists Robert Porter and Cobie Brinkman surgically implanted microelectrodes in the SMA of a monkey and discovered that about one tenth of a second before the monkey pulled a lever to obtain food, the cells in its SMA fired, well before the cells in the motor cortex, which is the portion of the brain concerned with muscular movement.

In the 1960s, neurophysiologists Hans Kornhuber and Luder Deecke developed a method for measuring minute electrical potentials occurring in the patient's scalp and they found a certain readiness potential; almost one second before carrying out a simple voluntary action, the brain displays a gradual increase in negative electrical potential. This increase is the brain's way of getting ready to make a voluntary movement, and Kornhuber and Deecke discovered that it was greatest in the SMA.

In 1980 a research group headed by neurophysiologists Nils Lassen and Per Roland of the University of Lund in Sweden used radioisotopic detection to monitor blood flow through the brain in relation to brain activity. They found SMA activity and motor area activity during voluntary activity. It was while performing a variation of the motor sequence test that they obtained their remarkably and controversial results. In a variation of the experiment called the 'internal programming test', the patient was asked to carry out the same difficult motor sequence test with no accompanying physical movement whatsoever. As expected, when patients performed this procedure, there was no motor area blood flow increase, whilst the SMA was activated almost as much as if movements had been performed. When it became habitual and could occur without conscious attention, the anticipatory activity in the SMA disappeared. Neurophysiologist Sir John Eccles, in reviewing this research, concluded: 'It is important to recognise that this burst of discharge of the observed SMA cell was not triggered by some other nerve cell of the SMA or elsewhere in the brain . . . So we have here an irrefutable demonstration that a mental act of intention initiates the burst of discharges of a nerve cell.' He also pointed out that it has been found out that different acts of mental intention initiate different patterns of neural discharge in the SMA. Eccles concluded that some resultant of complex code is involved and that the non-physical mind is actually 'playing' the 50 million or so neurones in the SMA region as if they were the keys to some sort of piano. These learned repertoires of sequential codes, Eccles believes, are the learned process of a lifetime.

Directed attention fixated on the SMA stimulates the brain to perform actions such as RS memes programmed into it by using this technique. You can remotely influence people by concentrating on their SMA and pulsing your desires into their brain. Once you learn how to light up their SMA with your biophysical field, that person is effectively under your command. This is a technique widely used by the military.

This occurs because every time you make the conscious decision to do something and carry it out, the SMA fires. By using DA you can do the same, thus getting yourself to do things you know you have to do, but could not get yourself to do before. Self-activation of the SMA is the best means of self-motivation and if done correctly is invariably successful. This technique can be used to boost RS capability. For RI practice (see glossary), use this technique on another person by projecting your biophysical field over their body. Then pulse your thoughts into their SMA until you learn to light it up on command.

As an exercise in programming your biophysical vehicle:

1. Use the relaxation programme described above to inculcate a theta state.

2. Fixate your awareness on the thalamus and focus the mental laser light of your DA on producing a mental screen in your mind's eye.

3. Visualise your biophysical body being made manifest in front of your mind's eye on the mental screen.

4. Intend the 'I' part of your attention – the epicentre of your DA, and the part of you that knows you are you – to enter your biophysical RS vehicle, which is the biophysical field trained to RS.

5. Intend your biophysical RS vehicle being programmed by your DA to carry out all the goals in the specific ways you wish it to operate. Use the above rules as an aid to 'programming'. Since it is your biophysical vehicle, programme it with the goal achievement programming you wish it to display – the RS of goals you wish to pursue as well as the site and people you wish to remotely sense in pursuit of these goals.

6. Allow your biophysical RS vehicle to begin initiating your goal-directed programming, scanning the sites and all the personnel of interest to your goals. It will automatically sense how to achieve your goals. Sparks of intuition will come to you or acausal synchronous events will allow your goals to be achieved by giving you the timing you need to achieve them.

7. Next, RS all future events connected with your goals to see how this programming of your biophysical vehicle influences your achievement of them.

As you can see, this basic methodology can be adapted by the RS student to suit his needs, and can be optimised by the person for his specific intents. As a further exercise in programming your SMA for RS, follow steps 1–5 above, then:

6. Visualise your SMA area of the brain programming your biophysical body to carry out this RS programming. In this way, your own brain can begin to link with your biophysical body to develop the synergy needed for proper RS.

7. Relax. Focus your directed attention on your thalamus. Now direct the mental laser of directed attention on the SMA.

8. Command your brain to switch off the brain stress system every time you practise RS. Programme the intent of accurate RS every time you focus your DA on the SMA.

Supraprogramming – the self-image

This is a construct of all the software you are running in your brain. Software, however acquired is a construct and therefore mutable, and can be changed to optimise your RS potential. Define (intend) how you wish to be and write it down clearly. Access the mind using DA and visualise the psiops abilities you wish to have.

The epicentre of directed attention in the mind–brain modem is in the supplementary motor area. This feeds a new programme into the brain and body's nervous system, causing it to be immediately implemented. So, visualise all the psiops attributes you really want to have, the RV/RS abilities you would like to have, then programme this software into the brain via the SMA.

Revised mental algorithms

1. Lateral thinking is a useful tool to see round problems. It is a non-linear way of thinking where ideas and acts not directly connected have indirect associations which can solve a problem that appears insoluble. For example, consider 'my business is infested with rats and I cannot use poison' (a simplistic example but it explains the point). We can use word association as lateral thinking to solve this problem: 'rat–black–hairy–smelly–fat–cat! – cat eats rat'. This solves our problem and shows that linear thinking isn't the only way to solve problems. RS awareness is aided by learning to think laterally. In remote sensing it is important that the data you get from your biophysical vehicle is allowed to enter your mind through free association.

   To try this, relax using the RS relaxation programme

described above, then:

a) Feed the person to be scanned into your biophysical vehicle using DA.

b) Allow your biophysical vehicle to align with the bio-physical body of the person being scanned.

c) Allow the biophysical vehicle to pick up information in any manner it wishes.

d) Let the biophysical vehicle return to the physical body. Allow the biophysical vehicle to download information into your brain by a method of non-linear programming which allows the information to enter your brain by a method of free association.

With this method, the biophysical vehicle can use non-linear data processing to upload information.

2. Negative feedback: use all setbacks to revise your RS prac-tice to minimise negative feedback. To do this, relax using the RS relaxation programme described above, then:

a) Use your DA to go over and revise all setbacks you have had in your RS practice session or at work.

b) Use DA to scan these people again.

c) Revise your methodology until you optimise your RS. By this method you can use error correction to hone your RS ability.

3. Positive feedback. Home in on triumphs to steer the fastest course to efficient RS – don't use success as an excuse to rest on your laurels.

Feed negative entropy into all aspects of your remote perception so all chaotic phenomena are driven from your RS. To do this, relax using the RS relaxation pro-gramme described above, then:

a) Use DA to concentrate your mental laser of awareness on your biophysical body.

b) Use DA to intend your biophysical vehicle to the countryside.

c) Allow your biophysical vehicle to suck up adaptive energy from the biophysical mantle of the countryside.

e) Use this adaptive energy to build your biophysical body, concentrating on all your experiences of scanning and empathy that were correct.

Psiops applications: principles of motivation

Just as each of us imagines how we look to other people, so does a company or organisation. This corporate self-image may not correspond to that which top management would want the organisation to have. The real self-image is that which is promoted by idle talk in coffee breaks. It is shaped mostly by gossip. Memes are the body of company culture.

Gossip tends to be thought of as useless, or worse, but it cannot be ignored, since almost three-quarters of all conversation consists of gossip. It is the principal medium through which company culture is propagated. The gossip which shapes a corporate culture is exactly analogous to the internal gossip which each of us uses to sustain our personal self-image throughout our lives; we are constantly talking to ourselves to tell ourselves who we are. Our picture of ourselves is sustained by our 'internal gossip'.

As we have seen, these self-images carry embedded in them an emotional overtone which is very powerful. Negative emotional overtones drive, and are perpetuated by, the destructive feedback cycle; likewise, positive emotional overtones drive a cycle of success. Both are self-sustaining and feed on themselves. The group internal models, taken with their emotional overtones, comprise the company culture. Once established, because it is self-perpetuating, a company culture is almost impossible to change.

Where, then, should an organisation begin? Success certainly breeds success, so, similarly, the principles can be applied to the group. In addition, however, when we are dealing with groups, the process can be further enhanced by applying the principles of peer pressure.

Principle 1: Every crisis has a positive side
A crisis provides opportunities for the manager to gain ground. A setback is a good teacher, and a reminder that established ideas and practices need to change. When disasters come, look for the benefits that can be extracted from them. RV and RS of the actual situation automatically lead to RV of scenarios to alleviate the problem. The first principle of psiops motivation is based on the idea that we do not feel threatened if we can pigeon-hole people or ideas. All of us pigeon-hole, if we can. We label and categorise all our experiences and observations. It makes data easier to handle. Since we do this naturally, we can use it to our advantage. This principle relies upon converting stress into a useful driving force.

Principle 2: Self-esteem is the basis of all human endeavour
Value your workers and allow their self-esteem to grow. They will not let you down as they develop; on the contrary, they will give you esteem for giving them space for growth. With empathic awareness this ability naturally comes into being.

The second principle deliberately seeks to induce positive

feelings. As we have seen before, the feelings that we experience are affected by our level of stress. Increasing the self-esteem of an individual or group automatically quenches the negative attitudes and animates any latent feelings of worth, thus setting up the positive cycle. This acts directly on the brain, releasing 'feelgood' hormones. Once established, gossip propagates and perpetuates this force which helps to drive the positive cycle.

Principle 3: Simulate success in the organisation at all times.
Since cause produces effect, the performance of the company is enhanced by rehearsing actual situations in a positive light. Do this on your own mental screen before actualising the success. This principle harnesses the capacity of people to work together on complex tasks in groups.

Principle 4: Everyone needs purpose
Give proper purpose to an organisation and its performance will improve dramatically. People with a purpose do not give up. They achieve their goals no matter what it takes. Give yourself purpose. Give it to your staff and your firm will thrive. Purpose is the motivating power behind achievement. By using RS one can spot what drives people and learn to use it in your business. This principle uses the concept of goal direction, promoting the positive feedback cycle. Managers who share the same goal will ignore personal conflicts and incompatibilities. It is of the utmost importance to corporate culture to ensure that all the personnel share the same large-scale, long-term goals. It is the duty of top management to make sure that they do.

Grass-roots support is essential. It requires free-flowing vertical feedback from staff to managers and from managers to top executives, and a feeling that top executives are there to implement mutually agreed goals for the common good. As we have already seen, the company culture is staff-driven, whilst top executives provide the infrastructure, and, being well informed about the outside world, implement new modes of operation as required. Managers, as intermediaries, are there to serve the staff and make sure that the job gets done. As part of this task, they must constantly strive to improve flexibility and reaction time. In our changing times, RS gives the extra capability to stay ahead.

Principle 5: Optimism – the observer affects reality

Observers with a positive frame of mind create positive events around themselves. Well-founded positive attitudes are contagious. Happy, healthy-minded employees perform best. Using RS to really understand employees' minds is the key to motivation – a natural ability of a born leader. We will discuss leadership skill in later chapters – this translates into success.

Although we have attempted to identify separate motivational principles, they are really all just aspects of one thing. This principle concerns the outlook of the organisation. This, too, is an aspect of how people view the organisation and what they feel about it.

The self-starting psiops manager should use the motivational principles set out above as a checklist. Consider how you could apply all five motivational principles to your business and what they might help it to achieve. If this seems remote and abstract, consider first, as an example, how the five motivational principles helped the Allies to win the Second World War. Things looked bleak in 1940, and worse still after Pearl Harbor, but when Hitler had overrun Europe and the Japanese had conquered the Far East, all five of these motivational principles could be seen at work. And, as a bonus, a powerful positive feedback cycle was set in train. The six years of the war witnessed technological advances which would otherwise have taken a generation to achieve. The cycle established at that time continues to drive the world economy 50 years later.

Enhancing the company culture by use of psiops

The principles of motivation have to be applied to implement change. The principles should be considered at the level of the individual – the forward-looking manager or keen member of staff. But a group is greater than the sum of its individual members. Now, we can understand how the motivational principles enable them to act on the entire group. In essence this is the simplest type of remote influencing. A contagious meme is generated, then the group is infected with this biophysical energy thoughtform which grows within them like a virus. This can be understood by remote viewing the different aspects of company culture. Questions to find the answers to, and principles to follow, include:

1. What are the core competencies of the company? What are the best aspects of the organisation? There are always some positive aspects – even in the most demoralised of organisations. The fact that you are interested in business applications of military psiops suggests that there is at least one individual in the company who is not sunk in complacency.

2. Eliminate the negative. The things that are wrong with

the company must be honestly confronted. List them and root them out. This is not easy, but acknowledging the problem is half the battle. Destroying negative memes is vital to releasing energy that can be used to empower the psiops company.

3. Establish a network of managers who accept the need to provide those beneath them in the hierarchy with whatever they need to do their job. Training them in the psiops way is a starting point.

4 Establish a matrix of staff cells, acting as far as possible on their own initiative. This promotes subsidiarity within the organisation, with activities taking place in groups of optimal size. Productivity is thereby raised through several mechanisms, acting in concert. Special forces use four-man cells. These are expanded in units of four.

The four steps described above distil the best aspects of company culture. Now, these are activated by the principles of motivation to initiate a positive feedback cycle which helps the company achieve its long term goals. Once established, this cycle feeds on itself and is therefore self-perpetuating. Eventually the positive feedback cycle becomes the company culture.

5 The positive feedback cycle incubates the microclimates of opportunity and helps to bring the company goals to fruition.

6 The positive feedback cycle also brings about self-renewal

of the company culture and its core – the things it does best – which enabled the company to grow in the past.

Now that the organisation is on the right path, steady improvement is possible: this feeds into the company culture, adding to those aspects of the organisation whatever is needed for growth.

What people do also affects the company culture. Staff in an organisation perform the same kind of operation repeatedly, and their way of doing things is spread by a variety of means such as gossip and peer pressure. Working practices, good or bad, are contagious. Company culture cannot be divorced from the activities normally carried out by the organisation and the way that those activities are performed. The process is reflexive; optimising these activities naturally optimises company culture. RS-capable managers will have a pivotal effect on this.

Company culture has no purpose other than to achieve mutually agreed goals – those derived from the microclimates of opportunity, as well as the normal core aims such as increasing market share, etc. Since the positive feedback cycle thrives on goal direction, the more goals that are fed in, the better the results, and the more the cycle is reinforced. Here we see in action the law of increasing returns which we came across earlier. Furthermore, once a positive feedback cycle gets under way, goals other than those which are consonant with the common good will never gain currency.

Training methods in psiops

Training methods form an integral part of psiops. Because the six principles of training work together and exploit different aspects of the ideas discussed in previous chapters, there is naturally some overlap between them. If you are training others in psiops, here are six important points:

1. Ready-state priming

This means getting people in the right frame of mind to receive new material. Knowledge of RS allows the trainer to know the mind set of his trainees, thus to enable an empathic approach to training. This boosts the self-worth of the pupils and maximises the abilities of the trainees.

a) Make the pupils feel at ease to help them absorb what is being taught. Empathic awareness is the key.

b) Impart a positive emotional feeling and content into the presentation so that the good feelings are recovered when the material is recalled.

c) Make sure that the positive feedback cycle is working. To this end:
   i) Make the lecture environment as congenial as possible; select a pleasant room, with attractive decor and comfortable chairs, and be generous with creature comforts – good quality coffee and biscuits are important, for example.
   ii) Impart a personal feeling to the meeting. Address your pupils by name and engage them in easy conversation. This relieves anxiety.

d) Use the technique of DA to involve your pupils. When they come to recall what you taught them, they then pass, without effort, into this same state of DA, which increases efficiency and reduces stress.

2. Stimulate attention

Training is impossible unless you secure and maintain the attention of those you are teaching. On the other hand, they must be kept relaxed as the alpha state is best for information retention.

a) Remember that pupils follow the teacher. If the teacher is relaxed, confident, knows the subject and has a happy demeanour, the pupils will absorb similar feelings.

b) Pay attention to your voice. Changes in rhythm and volume help to maintain the listeners' attention – this was one of the key discoveries of Bulgarian and Russian research into superlearning (super-fast learning).

c) Engage as many avenues of attention as possible. Make use of a variety of media. In addition to ordinary speech, exploit the possibilities of overhead projection slides, written text and diagrams, models, film, and video, and practical demonstrations and experiments in which the students can participate.

d) Encourage students to use the technique of DA as they interact with you. They should not be dumb listeners but active participants. Inculcate the benefits of relaxed, focused attention.

3. Systemisation

Make the material easy to assimilate. Define it rigidly; at best, it could be presented just as it might be for rote learning by young children. This pleases the reptilian complex in the brain and keeps down stress levels.

a) Try to impart the material step by step, taking the form of clearly defined instructions which could be passed on to someone else.

b) Keep the number of steps to a minimum. Four or five is the optimum.

c) Present the material in a deliberate and orderly way. This helps remembering, recall and implementation, because methodical and systematic ways of doing things are reassuring and not stressful.

d) Present all new material as no more than a continuation and extension of what has been done before. People become attached to old things and established ways of acting. We resist change. On the other hand, everyone likes to improve the old, to prove that it is better than some new-fangled idea. Since very little in the world is radically new, we can apply this approach to almost anything. If the new thing really is radically new, use imagination to link it to the past. This approach soothes the reptilian complex – the detonator of stress – making the pupil feel relaxed with the material.

e) Linking new initiatives to the past also avoids the danger of introducing practices which fail to mesh, which do not fit in to the way that the organisation works and might be entirely inappropriate.

f) Use texts and pictures that stimulate memory by connecting the new material with what is already known.

Stories, anecdotes and old familiar sayings all help to put a message across and get it to stick.

4. Relaxed mode attention
This is the ideal state for teachers and pupils. They are happy, relaxed and receptive.

a) Cut down anxiety by having clearly defined goals.

b) A relaxed and confident lecturer naturally brings people into a state of directed attention, holding their attention.

c) Keep sessions short. Have regular breaks. Steer pupils away from the habit of working hard when they are listening to you. Your material should be in well-organised written form so that students are not distracted from what you are saying by having to take notes.

d) Appreciate that people are naturally in a stressed condition, which will become embedded in what you are teaching them if you do not do something about it. Your pupils' emotional state during your training sessions is as important as what you are actually trying to teach them. Put your pupils in a relaxed state of mind. If you engender feelings of wellbeing, these will be remembered along with the material. This will stimulate your students to implement the new management initiatives.

5. Directed attention
Directed attention has already been mentioned as a relaxed-but-focused state, when brain activity, as measured on monitoring equipment, shows minimal beta-wave

activity, high alpha and theta-wave activity, and both the left and the right halves of the brain working together. Thinking like this is more efficient and uses less energy; we can really get to grip with problems. Time seems to pass more slowly, allowing us more time for everything.

Unfortunately, our attention is drawn by so many distractions that our brains are normally saturated by beta waves. We experience this as 'busy thinking'; we worry about problems and try to figure them out in a step-by-step logical sequence. In the meantime, our attention is drawn away from the people and things around us, which might well give us cues about what has to be done. Events pass us by. In directed attention, we fix our attention in a relaxed manner on one specific event or activity in our immediate environment or in our mind's eye. This allows the brain to do whatever thinking happens to be needed at the time, without deliberate effort on our part. Thinking ahead in a disciplined way is a valuable exercise. Here are five rules for thinking ahead in directed attention:

a) Decide what is important now, and what is important to the long-term future of the organisation using RV and RS.

b) Identify the key factors affecting the local environment of the organisation and the driving forces behind these using RV/RS. Rank their effects in order of importance and degree of uncertainty. Do not waste time and energy in thinking about remote possibilities or things which do not matter.

c) Select scenarios, then RV each one.

d) Consider implications: how does the organisation change with RV scenarios, and how are the important factors within the organisation affected? Can the organisation survive worst-case scenarios?

e) Use the principles of psiops management to consider possible alternatives for your organisation by using RV of possible futures. What degree of flexibility is required to enable it to survive the worst-case scenario and prosper in better circumstances? Detailed remote viewing of the future then offers the best route to success. More on the protocols of future RV in Chapter Nine.

6. Visualisation

The more mental images that are attached to material taught, the better it is remembered. Imagery and imagination have immense power – feed information in this way into the hypothalamus and from there by internal RS into one's memory palace. Use visualisation not only to propagate new management initiatives, but also to implement the material.

a) Develop the habit of connecting information with positive mental images using pictures, stories and anecdotes, or anything which places what you are trying to teach or learn within a familiar framework. The same principle applies, of course, if you yourself are trying to learn new material. Aim to connect what you are being taught with something that is part of your familiar experience. Use RS to add it to your memory palace.

b) Learn how to visualise with your eyes open. It integrates the right half of the brain (which deals with acts of imagining) with the left side (which deals with reading, writing and calculation). This relaxes the mind and enhances efficiency.

c) During meetings, involve others with imagery; ask them to picture what you are talking about.

d) Remember that visual imagery is the most powerful, as sight is the most powerful and dominant of the senses. If the new management initiatives possess visual attributes, they will be remembered and put into effect. This is why company logos, vehicle liveries and so on can help bring the organisation into focus.

e) In the 'Cinema Screen' method of RV we use visualisation to build a mental screen upon which we project all our RV. The soundtrack to our mental cinema screen is the range of RS channels. One channel is used for our questions to the target to be sensed, the other the answers to our questions coming from the mind of the target. The target thinks they are talking to themselves, not a remote sensor. This method is the cornerstone of psiops management and serves as a suitable point to delve deeper into RS.

SEVEN

THE BRAIN–BODY MODEM

Directed attention epicentred on the thymus gland stimulates the immune system and raises the energy level of the body's life-force using adaptive energy – negative entropy. The more negative entropic force we have, the better our remote sensing.

Behavioural kinesiology (invented by US genius Dr Mark Diamond) shows how the environment effects our adaptive energy. When using this technique, directed attention on the thymus moves adaptive energy from this organ (where it is stored) around the body. For effective RS, we need our biophysical bodies to be charged up with enough adaptive energy to overcome the activation energy needed for RS.

Practical exercises

As an exercise, place your tongue on the soft palate; feeding negative entropy from the thymus store into the body raises one's energy levels so one is immune to outside negativity – excellent for business meetings and confrontations. It is also a good start-up mode for RS. Feed adaptive energy into the biophysical body from the thymus, using DA. Reduce entropy in one's body and enhancing life-force, via DA fixated on negative entropy.

Directed attention focused on the thymus of the person you wish to remotely sense boosts RS. It can also cause their physical, rather than mental, control.

Visualising your target to be more relaxed, while you remotely sense them, will increase the probability of your successful scanning of him or her.

Being able to remotely sense adaptive energy in the people you are scanning is vital for future developments. To this end, follow the exercises below to get a feel for adaptive energy in others. This trains your biophysical fields to recognise biophysical energy in others.

Remote sensing and adaptive energy

1. Test life-force using muscle testing. The subject stands, right arm at their side, left arm parallel to their shoulders, elbow straight. Facing the subject, place your left hand on their right shoulder to steady them; then place your right hand on the subject's extended arm above the wrist. Tell the subject you are going to push down on their arm and for them to resist. Now push down on their arm quickly and firmly; push hard enough to test the spring and bounce in the muscle but not hard enough to cause fatigue. Perform the test again as the subject eats some white sugar and/or drinks coffee, listens to heavy rock music, stares at a fluorescent light or thinks of an unpleasant situation. You will find in the above cases that the muscle tested is weakened by the stressor unless the person tested has high adaptive energy (which is very rare).

2. Stimulate the thymus gland and other endocrine gland using a thymus thump (which involves lightly tapping

the thymus) and directed attention. This also boosts the immune system. The subject places the fingertips of their free hand on the skin over the point where the second rib joins the breast bone (the sternmanubrial joint), directly over the thymus gland. As the subject does this, test the indicator muscle as above.

If the subject tests strong, all is okay; if the muscle tests weak this means the energy supply to the subject's thymus gland is insufficient and or the thymus (immune system) is underactive. The first result shows adaptive energy is being used to maintain the integrity of the organism; the second result shows the person's adaptive energy is being used to fight stress and maintain functioning in the outside world at the expense of the body. We can test any stressor using the above method and get one of the following results:

a) Not affected by stimulus.
b) Stimulus weakens the thymus gland and uses up adaptive energy.
c) The stimulus is so detrimental that the muscle feels weak even without being touched.

For effective RS it is vital that the operator learns to store all their adaptive energy in his thymus, so it can be used by the biophysical body for RS and is not wasted. This means we must learn to be in the state where we are unaffected by the stimulus for RS.

3. Try to centre left–right brain hemispheres. A subject with strong indicator muscle – which is any muscle whose life-force is being tested for stimuli – places the palm of their right hand approximately two inches

away from the left side of their head. If they have balanced brain hemispheres the muscle will test strong, as it will also remain strong when they place the palm of the right hand opposite their right ear. This tests the respectivel; activity of left and right brain hemispheres. If the subject is 'normal' the indicator muscle will test weak whilst testing the left hemisphere. This is dominant in Western people, showing the preponderance of linear thinking in the brain. Get the subject to do a mathematical problem in their head. Immediately, upon placing the palm of the right hand near the left side of the head the indicator muscle will go weak. This is not so with the right hand near the right side of the head – in fact, we get the opposite result.

To balance hemispheres in the brain, visualise left and right parts of the brain in harmony. This simple act of visualisation has the same effect as a thymus thump and balances hemispheres, making you more efficient and enabling you to handle stress. Balanced hemispheres are useful for RS as they amplify the phenomena. They also allow the brain the ability to interact with your own biophysical field in an optimal manner.

4. Take energy breaks frequently to charge your body. To do this, one can attune oneself to harmonius high negative entropy (landscape paintings, music, poems), and store this life-force by using DA to channel it into your thymus. This boosts the RS vehicle.

5. Maintain correct posture: the Alexander Technique boosts the adaptive energy available for RS, as energy is

not being wasted in tense musculature and constricted vertebrae.

6. Concentrate DA on past events. After stressful situations, rerun the situation in a positive light so it loses its power as a stressor, and thus does not drain your adaptive energy or act as a block to RS.

7. Place your tongue on the 'centering button' whilst practising all RS. This is situated in the palate, just behind the front teeth, on the roof of your mouth, Doing this gives a boost to the energy available for all RS.

8. Concentrate DA on positive programming, epicentred on the thymus brain–body modem. This increases adaptive energy available for RS. When inputting positive RS amplifying memes, this methodology should be followed to programme these memes into your biophysical field as data bits in the adaptive energy being channelled from your thymus to your biophysical body.

9. Direct your attention on your own SMA using DA, activating it with the intent of RS. Adaptive energy will test strong by muscle testing every time you think of that intent. This methodology should be followed when reprogramming your biophysical body, editing negative memes and inputting positive memes.

10. Epicentre your attention on your thymus using DA. Mentally feed energy into it and the muscles will test

strong afterward no matter what the stressor. This technique channels energy into the biophysical field phenomena used for RS.

11. Direct your attention on your target's SMA using RS. Show the effect of the ideas you scanned in to the subject's mind via the SMA. Weaken or strengthen their muscles according to your RI. Test the effects by muscle testing the person. In this you can correlate the SMA activity with muscle strength. This idea can be developed as an aid to RS or RI.

12. Direct your attention on their thymus as you mentally ask the person a question. If they lie, testing this person will show their adaptive energy has been lowered – thus their indicator muscle tests weak. This technique is another cornerstone of RS, as one can do this on the target in ones mind's eye without recourse to physically touching the person. By this method, one can psychically question anyone, anywhere in the world. Since there is no simple effective defence, no secret can remain secret, no lie can remain hidden to the power of RS. All military defence protocols are based on blocking the technical remote viewing protocols developed for the CIA and DIA.

To conclude, adaptive energy must be linked with RS for effective scanning.

The genius factor

Use directed attention to access states of deep relaxation, passing through the subconscious into the unconscious. It can also be used as a link to normal consciousness so that conscious, unconscious, and subconscious are in one's DA. To do this, it helps if you colour-code conscious white, subconscious black and unconscious blue. Here are some examples of DA's uses in this context:

1. Gut feelings, intuition and hunches are correct when they come from the unconscious, as it is a subset of the collective unconscious, which holds the sum total of human knowledge. One can colour code biophysical fields to show their intent. Use DA to internally RS your consciousness. Code the unconscious blue, subconsious black, as well as linking the colours with truth (blue) and deception (black). Use internal RS to analyse any thought in your head. RS of people's minds using this technique allows you to see where the idea set your biophysical body picked up came from. Using the above criteria to evaluate them can prove helpful in downloading this information into your brain in a meaningful manner.

2. Use DA to switch off the data stream – the internal chatter in your mind – to cease thought. This leads to new ideas surfacing from unconscious and collective unconscious which is the repository of creative thought. This also boosts RS and is amplified by the cinema screen method; using RS data to fill your mental screen, you watch another person's thoughts projected onto your thalamus by DA.

3. Unlock hidden potential that you never know you had. Relax, focus DA on a specific intent on your cinema screen, then let go and await the result. This method is useful for scanning people to see if they have the same

specific intent as you, (as your own intent will align with an identical one in their head which can be seen while scanning). This is useful for scanning large numbers of people for specific intents: agreement with a board decision, departmental change, promoting you, or in the negative case an informer, spy or wrecker (or disruptive element).

4. One can scan people for similar memories by using the same methodology as above. By using directed attention on forgotten memory you can let go of intent and await the memory which will come to you at a future date.

5. Directed attention focused on the hindbrain (or reptilian brain system) leads to a massive increase in data flow to the cerebral cortex and your consciousness. This information contains, among other things:
   a) Visual clues as to other people's true mental state (from subtle clues in their body language among other things), thus one knows if one is being lied to.
   b) An increase in one's empathic abilities, so one can get into the head of one's colleagues, staff and competitors.
   c) Ideas will pop into one's head which give you an almost precognitive view of the world – due to the unfiltered data which our forebrain (or cortex) can process to give us enhanced perception.

Plan of action:
1. Learn to wake up lucidly by being in the theta state every time one carries out RS. Do not be asleep, as

normal people tend to be, but develop RS. Learn to awaken your true potential, fully activating software of success (memes) to boost RS/RV and the suprapro-gramme thereof. Lucid waking is analogous to lucid dreaming and is the requisite state for RS/RV.

2. Become a centre of theta consciousness in your busi-ness: gather information by use of RS on all your business associates and clients. Give out creative new information that promotes your business by using tele-pathic hypnosis to input these ideas into other people's minds (negative entropy can be added to idea to make it more successful). This can be done by con-tacting the unconscious of clients via directed attention on the RS of person of interest.

3. Change environment; eliminate the negative and accen-tuate the positive by developing use of psiops memes and memetic science.

4. Give a word of praise to all your employees when they perform well. Use RS to empathise with them, and know how they feel. Use scanning to read their minds and RI to input your own ideas, so they look upon them favourably.

5. Use power spots of negative entropy to charge up your adaptive energy for RS and use behavioural kinesiol-ogy (see glossary) to conserve it. These power spots are usually ancient ruins, henges, mounds or places with many ley lines. Once you feel replete, programme your brain using the SMA modem to avoid stressors and to

habituate behaviour that does not drain your adaptive energy. Use self muscle testing to check up on your adaptive energy by touching your thymus with one hand and pressing down on the elbow of that hand with the opposite hand's finger, to test the 'bounce' of that muscle.

6. Replicate your actions down the chain of employees by using RS to input your own memes into them.

7. Have regular workshops for your staff during which you manifest your own memes in their perception by talking about them.

8. Never treat any one in your organisation as an enemy – empathise with all employees. Use RS to scan them and input the tailored meme by use of RI, that will make them compliant to your ideas.

9. See all problems as negative feedback to enable you to reach your goal – you must react to reach your goal, but in a positive manner using RS as a tool and RI to sway people your way. Remember the mind has no firewalls – so be careful you are not influenced by others in this manner.

Goal direction

Since the *locus coeruleus* is not switched off by the body, this centre of the brain constantly keeps the brain stress system in an activated state. It is up to the individual to turn off this debilitating effect by introducing the above behaviour into their working environment and, more importantly, to use one of the characteristics of the reptilian brain to switch it off. This characteristic is the goal-orientated nature of the reptilian brain.

An RS operator is totally goal-directed, ignoring stressors and conflicts that have no bearing on his or her goals.

Psiops: the cycle of success to stimulate life-force in a business

How can we put into practice what we have already said about energising, so it applies to a business to stimulate success? It is easier said than done, because nobody likes change. One can think of success as the starter motor for a positive cycle. Success then breeds success. One small success leads to another; start with modest goals, take one day at a time and cultivate those habits which bring success. Many millionaires, for example, have tapped into enough of the principles of success to make the entire system work in their favour. Success is a form of life-force or adaptive energy. This chapter has been about monitoring and charging the individual with life-force.

How do we change businesses? How can a cycle of success be set in motion in a business? Use remote viewing to find the cycle of success in your mind's eye, the reality where your business works. Pupils learning to swim would be discouraged if they had not managed to swim a single stroke after a few visits to the pool. But if they have managed to swim just a yard or two at the end of the first lesson, future visits will be eagerly awaited and before long they will be proficient swimmers. To motivate people to make progress, the instructor must understand and apply this principle: pupils must gain an experience of success from the start.

In psiops management, we have brought together a collection of some of the most effective and proven principles of success. Millionaires and other successful people use only a few of these principles. But since the principles of success work synergistically, when they are used together, the benefits multiply rather than just add. Applying these principles at work will have dramatic effects.

As recently as the 1950s, technologies were good for perhaps 20 years; in the 21st century, new technologies can come along every year. If machinery and the skills that go with them become obsolete so quickly, all that companies possess are their staff, which now have to be thought of as its capital. And if people are to attain their full potential, staff and managers must be helped to understand not only what is going on in their heads, but also the simple principles outlined below which they can use to help themselves and the organisation to do their best.

Principles of psiops

The first principle of psiops is that irrelevant thinking, pettiness and anger get in the way of this energy-charging process. A familiar example of this is after an argument, when we keep on thinking about what we ought to have said. We all make decisions in anger which make us feel weak afterwards; we would not have made them had we been in a calmer frame of mind:

1. **Eliminate everything negative or obsolete to make room for success**. Anything negative drains you of your energy. If the negative thinking is dropped, the energy it was consuming can be used for producing positive memes which bring success.

The second principle of psiops deals with having to clearly define, within one's head, what goals one wishes to achieve. We can take advantage of the mind's peculiar ability to reflect on a problem and let the solution come to mind later on, of its own accord. Use remote viewing to find the solution and internal RS to define the question:

2. Therefore to succeed, **know your goals, define them clearly and write them down in your mind's eye**, using the power of DA to focus on your mental cinema screen (the mind's eye view of your awareness now systematised onto a screen). Then use remote viewing in the same manner to see how you can achieve them.

The third principle of psiops exploits the fact that people copy each other in speech, tone of voice, body language and other signals – memes are contagious:

3. Remember that **what you give, you get**. It is a universal principal that like action begets like action.

The fourth principle of psiops uses the power of the imagination to think ahead. A wise manager takes advantage of this. Use RV/RS to look into the future:

4. **Visualise your goals as if they have already been achieved**. Acting as if you were successful brings success. Do this on your mental cinema screen.

The fifth principle of psiops relates to speech. It is no use saying something in a tone of voice which conveys another message altogether:

5. **As you speak, so shall it be**. Listen to the sound of your own voice and never vocalise what you do not want to happen. Likewise, use RI to speak into the minds of your targets in a firm, declarative voice to programme them to your will.

Principles six and seven of psiops are about bringing ideas to fruition.

6. **If you have to do something, do not delay but do it immediately**; if you don't need to do it, don't.

7. **Do what you have to do no matter what it takes**. Only make commitments you are willing to honour; once you have made them always go through with them as long as they have to be done.

The eighth principle of psiops emphasises positive thoughts. Just as negative thoughts go round in the head, so can positive ones. This keeps the mind focused on the goal even when the person is subject to heavy resistance opposing that goal. It enables the person or organisation to wear down the opposition. Use RI to project your goal into the minds of your enemies so they unwittingly aid you. Turn on their SMA as you do this.

8. **Perseverance: never, ever give up**. Repeat your attempts at intervals until you have carried them out. Likewise with RI, repeat the protocol until your target does as you wish. At first it may take many attempts, but as you get more energy, it will take fewer and fewer.

The ninth principle of psiops comes back to the involve-
ment of people's thoughts on a goal, but this time acting as
a group:

9. **Connectedness: imagining the event you wish to
   manifest increases the likelihood that it will
   really happen**. Broadcast this potential event into the
   minds of your enemies, key players and your support-
   ers to build up the energy for its actually happening.
   This is done by building a meme that feeds off one
   hundred remotely influenced people to manifest your
   will. By this method the psiops manager can control
   local reality. Nurturing the physical and social links
   with the company and clients you wish to influence
   increases the chance that you will get what you want.
   Use the same technique for reality control as above,
   with a positive empathic meme as the thoughtform.

The tenth principle of psiops is about the power of group
working. Teamwork has an ordering effect, by injecting
fresh ideas and energy into people, organisations and situations:

10. **To achieve your intentions, tailor your actions to
    those of your colleagues and clients**. This converts
    a chaotic situation into one that can be predicted and
    has inherent order; amongst other benefits, everyone
    feels less anxious. By remote sensing your colleagues
    and clients you know their mindset and, with empathic
    awareness at your command, you can push the right
    buttons in their psyche to manipulate them to your
    way of thinking.

Many of the principles just described are familiar and long-established folk wisdom principles in the self-help tradition. What we have suggested shows there is a scientific basis behind this folk wisdom, and with this understanding it is easier to apply the principles and achieve results.

This is not, of course, to say that anything at all is possible. These principles will work only if the task attempted has a realistic chance of success. They will not turn you into an Olympic champion or a millionaire, unless you happen to have what it takes. A key to successful psiops management is to only embark on projects which are achievable. We can now see one of the reasons why this is so important. Failure leads to discouragement, and a cycle of success will never be established.

EIGHT

THE ART OF WAR IN BUSINESS

One can regard business as a form of war. The US and UK use their Echelon spy-supersystem to hoover up all world communication so US and UK firms can benefit from inside intelligence. The National Security Agency, the organisation that carries this economic warfare out, is the largest intelligence agency in the world. Similarly MI4, the UK's economic intelligence agency, is the largest UK intelligence agency and the most secret. It is referred to colloquially as the 'thought police' and it monitors all UK non-military activity from art to science. All intelligence agents are able to hide their emotions behind a mask of good manners and never give away their real intentions. Business to them is war, and they inveigle themselves into the enemy camp to gain intelligence. At present France and Germany are the main targets of MI4 and the NSA as they could be said to represent the old Europe that stands in the way of anglo-American power. To combat this high level of business warfare by intelligence agencies, RS is useful as you can scan all the people you come into contact with to see what their true intentions are.

Main weapons: Russian doll reality attack
This is a means of selling your competitor a false image of you and your company, which not only keeps your true

position hidden but which drains his or her adaptive energy so they weaken as the battle goes on. Use directed attention to empower RS and study data about your business situation and players, as in this state you can quickly assimilate vast amounts of information. Use mental simulation of possible scenarios, then use RV to see how they run in the future: this helps construct the optimum business scenario to maximise your position with respect to getting your enemy to do what you want. Construct layer upon layer of data that backs this chosen viewpoint (rather like statisticians do), reinforce it with 'facts' chosen to give a skeleton to the data; then 'sweeten' the picture in such a way as to boost your opponents' self-importance and enhance it with an overview of what your enemies want to see. Your rivals take themselves with a deadly seriousness the RS adept do not. To this end use the following tools:

a) Control of RV/RS/RI to manoeuvre your enemy onto your battlefield.

b) Discipline – to ignore their petty attacks.

c) Forbearance – to not lash out and harm yourself.

d) Timing – to use RV and RS of the future to find when your opponent will be most vulnerable to strike the mortal blow to their business.

e) Will – manipulate reality using RI to succeed. This involves the body-environment modem (BEM), which is located in the lumbar plexus, a nerve centre of the autonomic nervous system and is connected to the gut and the biophysical body.

Gut feelings about your surroundings and any situation you are in comes from the BEM. It gives you information about the people involved on an empathic level and as such – since it bypasses your intellect – it is difficult to deceive. To access the BEM relax and use DA on your lumbar plexus, which lies behind your navel. This is the hara upon which martial artists concentrate their energy and attention and from which all their movements derive.

When you have fixated your directed attention on the BEM you will get feelings about the 'vibes' around you. Further to this, if you visualise the specific situation you wish to evaluate and/or change, gut feeling will come to you which will invariably be right. To change the specific situation to your benefit, use DA fixated on this point; input the outcome you wish to occur, then focus this feeling on a picture (actual and/or in your mind's eye) of the person or event you wish to alter. Doing this will affect the probability of the outcome being in your favour, and in the long-term will so affect the odds that the forthcoming event manifests to your benefit.

This is one of the key techniques of RS and should be practised until you can use RS to get a gut feeling/intuition about any person or situation. This ability is honed in life or death situations to a high art.

Main weapons: Russian doll reality defence

At some time or other we have convinced ourselves of something or other which has been totally wrong but which we spent vast amounts of time and energy upholding, building layers and layers of spurious data to uphold our false viewpoint. These deleterious operating procedures must be cleared out of our systems before we can be sure we are ready to deal with the mass of false or incomplete data sent our way in business; to this end use the opposite of the steps above to defend against the Russian doll reality.

Main weapons: negative memes and data attack

Group data into difficult-to-digest lumps – loops that bring your rivals back to square one. Create data which is so constructed as to suck one's enemies into a strange attractor that produces information loss as it is assimilated and therefore reduces competitors' knowledge of your situation. These types of memes are perfect to construct if you wish to stop other people scanning your brain and biophysical vehicle. I use this to bombard the intelligence agencies with volumes of rubbish information so they never know where my research has led me, what its nature is and how far I have developed RV science. For that reason I never have written down research notes, which for a scientist is a cardinal sin. Anything you wish to keep secret should never be recorded. To this end, you could use negative memes that erode the true picture of you in your competitor's awareness through disinformation. There are three types of negative memes (or virus programmes) to be discussed (although, due to their potency, they are not recommended):

a) Hidden memes, which do not show up on normal scanning techniques but which cause the software of your
   enemy to be corrupted, in this case his or her biophysical fields and brain. This is very useful to use on military
   remote viewers who come a-calling.

b) Multi-sequential virus programmes that can be initiated by hundreds of different combinations of input into the software in which they are hidden, in this case your bio-physical fields and brain. Placing memes in your energy field that latch on to anyone entering your psychic-space for information. These memes can be designed to do anything to the attacker.

c) Hardware direct virus programmes. These bypass the software defences using pathways originally put there by the software programmer for easy access. These memes attack the brain of the telepath scanning you without their biophysical field being aware a memetic virus is present. This type of virus will be immune to all defences except psycrystals – see my web site www.rvscience.com for full information.

Most common hardware direct virus programmes are the pathogenic viruses that make people ill; these can be countered by boosting the immune system via the mind–body modem, the thymus and the use of vitamins to raise one's adaptive energy. They do this primarily by reducing oxidative stress on the body caused by free radicals. For this purpose the most important are:

Vitamin C: 1,000mg doses.
Vitamin E: 1,000i.u. doses.
Selenium: 200mcg doses.

Main weapons: negative memes and data defence
You should he aware of memetic virus programmes in your own being which remain hidden and are initiated by stimuli

from your past, causing illness, mental and or physical impairment. It is essential for the RS adept to hunt them out and erase them completely. To this end, use DA to clean out all negative memes. Use the key point that though masters of disguise, memetic virus programmes are centres of chaos, and that lack of order shows up in your mind's eye as black vortices. When found, use the anti-virus programme of a white vortex rotating in the opposite direction to expunge them. This is a biophysical thoughtform opposite in polarity and intent to the virus programme. This is a must-do for people in the limelight who have many psychic attackers.

Main weapons: information – your powerful defensive business weapon!

It is essential to have your awareness unfiltered so you can gather information, using RS, of what your enemy is giving out unconsciously, but which tells you what he is really thinking and planning.

Use your opponents' operating procedures against them: Japanese businessmen use the strategies laid down in Miyamoto Mushashi's *A Book of Five Rings*, ('the Japanese answer to the Harvard MBA'). To counter this high-level business warfare – most of it hidden behind a façade – remote sense to scan the real intentions of business associates, clients and competitors as necessary. The following techniques (which can also be used as methods of attack, as described previously) are helpful:

1. Countermove: it is difficult for your enemy to fight you if they have a false impression of you and the actual situation, so feed your enemy false information and vast

amounts of useless information. Use his or her self-importance to feed his ego and lead him into carefully prepared Russian doll realities.

2. Feed your enemy with negative memes and information that occupy his time and will tire him out. The Japanese, in particular, have meetings for discussion throughout the day, thus they are susceptible to overload by data.

3. When your enemies attack your company, use Russian doll realities, 'virus' programmes (or negative memes) and information to overwhelm them, so they get sold a false image of your company and/or 'blow a fuse'. This is useful for anti-scanning.

Self-importance in business warfare

Self-importance and saving face are very important to all business people. The RS operator uses self-importance to enable him or her to reach his goals:

1. Lessening self-importance in yourself makes your ideas much more acceptable and increases your standing.

2. Realising self-importance in others can be used to your advantage. The more conditioned and unaware the mind is, the more easily it can be controlled. Self-importance is so useful because when you activate it in your competitor, you automatically run software derived from his or her past which inhibits original, critical thought processes. This is the perfect state for you to work on him using your command of

business warfare. The mastery of RS makes the above unbeatable.

Sell your opponents false necessities. Use their self-importance to amplify their false needs. Enter into your competitors' minds using their self-importance as an access for RS and feed them with what they want to hear. Convince them they control you without you knowing. Convince your opponents of things that don't really exist using Russian doll reality. Suck them into a chaotic attractor that amplifies their awareness of your RS illusion using positive and negative memes that weaken their power to resist the illusion.

I have found the above useful in enabling the only non–CIA or DIA expert in the field to give the public the real facts about remote viewing . . . while MI5 tries every dirty trick in the book to shut me up.

Memes of use in remote sensing
The RS operator should be aware of the following memes, or Basic Principles of Business Warfare:

1. Train like you plan to fight.

2. When in doubt use industrial strength deterrence.

3. Priorities are man–made not God made.

4. If it is stupid but works it is not stupid.

5. Always honour a threat.

6. Know when it is time to get the hell out of the battle.

7. The important things are always simple.

8. If you are up to your eyeballs in enemies you are in combat.

9. Never put your life in the hands of someone who is braver than you.

10. A plan never survives the first 30 seconds of combat.

11. Only turn to blow the opposition away; otherwise, run away and fight another day.

12. Know your opposition.

13. Always know how to get out of the battle zone.

14. The simple things are always hard.

In constructing your battle plan you should be aware of the following points, as by using DA you simulate the battlefield, battle and the goals you wish to achieve on your mental cinema screen. A good plan will take all of your goals into account and, like the physical basis of reality, will be such that no matter what your enemy does, only one event scenario ever occurs – your victory. Use future RV and RS to explore time-lines involved with every scenario until you get it right. Then implement your plan. If the situation changes, repeat the above protocols to redesign your plan.

The memetics of business warfare

To win the battle, the following memetics are used in the DA mental cinema screen simulation which will enhance your chances of victory. Use of the body-environment modem whilst running the simulation will further increase the probability of a successful outcome from linking your will with the energy fields around you; ie, plugging into the biophysical energy of the earth.

1. RS operators choose their own battlefield – never go into battle without knowing your surroundings – as uncovered by RV.

2. Discard everything that is unnecessary, whilst realising you should feed your enemies with false, trivial and misleading data to disguise and/or improve the probability of your goal coming to fruition.

3. Aim at simple reactions to negative feedback, apply all your concentration to the problem – decide whether the battle is necessary, and if you fight, do it to your last breath or not at all. Be willing and ready to make your last stand if and only if you have no choice but to fight. RV and RS allow you to perfect the above to your situation.

4. Relax, abandon yourself, fear nothing – this accesses the theta state necessary for psiops.

5. When faced with odds that cannot be dealt with, RS operators let their minds wander – they occupy their time with something else. This unglues reality, so the situation slides away from your enemy to you. Your enemy

needs you to acknowledge his reality to make it real for you – never do this.

6. RS operators compress time, for even an instant counts, and at the crucial time in negotiations a second is an eternity – an eternity that may decide the outcome. Entering the delta state (see glossary) allows the psiops experts to slow time and speed up mental processing times to out-think their opponents.

7. The RS operator never pushes himself to the fore, he works through people – the director behind the front men. A hidden manipulator is much more effective. The real rulers of the West are not the politicians but the elite who own the Bank of England, Federal Reserve, IRS, World Bank, IMF and so on.

8. Information is the ordinance of business warfare. Information is proportional to negative entropy; thus the more information you have, the less chaotic the situation, and the more able you are to predict the outcome of the business battle (which, if it is not imperative, do not enter into!) A remote sensing expert has all the information on his enemies because he can scan their minds for all their secrets. In this age, all intelligence agencies are obsolete because every secret can be scanned from them – make sure this is not the case with your business.

Thus the RS operator draws his competitor, buyer, the city, entrepreneur and the like onto a battleground of his choice – he forces himself to disregard what is not essential, whilst overloading the enemy with nonessentials. Put your business standing on the line with a decision if and only if you have no choice but to fight and your gut feeling is 100 per cent positive. Relax in order to regroup your resources, enter into a new and different mood of optimism and self-confidence with your fellow business people, compress time and never push yourself to the fore. At all times use directed attention on RS/RV to maximise your abilities. Gain all the information you can gather about the situation using RV/RS, realising that your subconscious is constantly accumulating subliminal information that borders on the miraculous. By accessing your unconscious, you can know from the collective unconscious what your business enemy wants to do.

Use RS in all this memetic technology to input and scan the people you are dealing with. Applying these memetic principles leads the RS operator to:

1. Not take themselves too seriously – develop your sense of humour.

2. Learn to have endless patience.

3. Learn to have an endless capacity to improvise.

4. Realise that consciousness can and does alter reality, as quantum physicists have known since the turn of the century.

5. Use directed attention, which amplifies your normal consciousness and RS – the more you use DA, the stronger your consciousness becomes.

6. Constantly fixating DA on your epicentre of attention strengthens the 'I' in you, making you more aware of the true you. In the process this allows the 'I' to take over the whole you, so you wake up in normal consciousness. This whole process makes your mind and body more powerful, and it gives you the ability to withstand tremendous stress levels.

7. The mind–brain modem, when used by a strong consciousness and which has through DA expanded the epicentre of attention to encompass the whole mind, can exert total control over the brain. Doing so allows you to achieve all your goals, by using RI to control your target's brain.

8. Likewise the brain–body modem activated by DA can be used to boost the adaptive energy level and immune system of the body to such a degree that disease is easily fought off and your body retains its youthful vigour.

9. Once this is done the principles of success memes should be studiously practised until they become habits; from then on all negative software will be so uncomfortable it will be discarded in oneself and bounced back to people who throw it at you.

10. The supraprogramme of the RS manager will change to mirror the above enhancements leading to a person that radiates success, has charisma and the magic touch.

11. The body–environment modem has some remarkable attributes when used by the RS operator, giving them

an empathic knowledge of what is really going on and allowing their will to conquer all.

12. The RS operator does not look for a fight but, when left with no choice, will ruthlessly apply the Art of War in Business memes and memetics to the problem, only fighting after simulating all possible outcomes using RV/RS, the memetic technology and the body–environment modem. The probability of events going the RS operator's way are as near unity (a statistical probability of one means that is the only possible outcome) as possible.

13. Once in the actual fight, use DA fixated on your epicentre of attention to visualise your battle plan and goal. Check the outcome with RV to optimise it. In the process activate your own mind–body modem so you are immune to being coerced into the position your enemy wants you in, and at the same time charge up your energy levels by linking your brain–body modem into them. At the end of a long meeting, you are still charged up whilst your enemy is tired and vulnerable to mistakes which you can use for victory.

14. Use a keyword or image that you have previously programmed to activate the above responses, which you have rerun again and again in your RV/RS mental simulations prior to the meeting (so they are an automatic response to the meeting). Thus, all you have to do is use mental biofeedback fixated on your keyword image in RS to keep all this previously prepared success programmes running, leaving you free to

conduct a normal meeting whilst the memetic software enhances your performance. This is rather similar to mantras, which keep the meditator in alpha.

In the next section you will come across a whole new way of working with RS in the memetic mode. The aim has been to teach you how to optimise your RS so that you can apply all your expert knowledge to your own business. Continual repetition of the above memetic material is needed until you are comfortable with it. Once this happens and you apply it rigorously, not only will you achieve your RS goals, you will feel marvellous as well, being the RS operator that is really you! Mastery of these protocols leads to the manager becoming a psiops-capable leader.

Psiops applications: C3I and leadership

As we have seen, the core concept of psiops is largely derived from black-ops (deniable) military practice. Real-time satellite surveillance, for example, allows commanders to see what is happening in the battle zone as events are actually happening. This takes much of the guess work from anticipating the enemy's intentions. Psiops managers can use remote viewing and sensing to get a better real-time capability than the military; scanning the minds of your competitors, customers and own key players, using the methods described in previous chapters, will make it quicker and easier to monitor the organisation, and so speed up the reaction time of the company. Real-time management is the goal.

But how ought managers to do their job in a psiops organisation? Is it enough to carry on as before, reinforcing their strengths and eliminating their weaknesses? Should the psiops manager just allow subordinates to get on with their jobs? Or should they play the hard taskmaster?

In the first case, staff follow the example of their manager. Diligent, competent managers are respected, and subordinates feel under an obligation to perform their duties. Yet there is still plenty of scope for the manager who is a hard but respected commander, and who believes in keeping staff under close supervision.

It seems, perhaps, that both the 'autonomous action' and 'control' scenarios described above can be effective. Which approach is successful depends on the personality of the manager and the nature of the task; factory workers can be closely supervised, but not truck drivers. But whether or not managers get the best or worst from their staff depends more on themselves than on the management system. The manager can use remote viewing of different scenarios to see which of their possible personae will be most effective, and RS to see if it clashes with staff in practice.

In the business world, natural selection is at work, weeding out the bad managers. But many bad managers survive by sycophancy – ass kissing. There is one type of organisation, however, where bad managers do not survive – the military. Fighting units which do not perform tend to get wiped out. This is not to say that the fortunes of war do not turn against the best of generals and their staff – and it is well known that armies in peacetime are apt to go flabby – but powerful forces of selection have been at work over many years in armies and military organisations, and, as a result, they know a lot about leadership. And so we have looked at some aspects of the military model of management, and have tried to adapt these to civilian life.

It would, of course, be ludicrous and inappropriate to impose an army-type regime on civilians. But there is one element which is peculiar to the military, yet which could be adapted to the commercial world: C3I – Command, Control, Communication and Intelligence. The attraction of C3I is that it is simple and easily understood. Let us examine the four components of C3I in detail.

Command

1. Command by example

Military commanders lead by example. Officers are expected to do everything that their men do, and more besides. An outstanding example is Colin Powell, who fought in Vietnam, crushed Iraq in the first Gulf war and then became US Secretary of State. Psiops managers also lead by example. The phrase 'don't do as I do, do as I tell you' has no place in their vocabulary. Managers earn respect by deeds, not words. Once respect has been earned, staff will try to live up to the high standard set by their own manager. Their own self-esteem will grow, as their standard of work rises and they feel proud of working for a first-class manager. If they lapse, they will feel guilty and uncomfortable. Here we see another example of a positive cycle; the actions of the manager stimulate the staff to achieve more.

2. Command by objective

Psiops managers are goal-oriented. Before setting out, military commanders plan their mission to the last detail. They then play out different scenarios to optimise the plan. Once the plan is settled upon, each individual is told what to do, and practises until it becomes second nature. When they go into combat, each knows exactly what task to perform, and the leaders have specific plans for contingencies.

Psiops managers, too, must always be clear about what they wish to achieve. They plan how to win their objective with meticulous care. Once the strategy is decided upon, they simulate the best and worst-case scenarios. Psiops managers accept that reality is harsh and that business has much in common with war; being able to RS the opponent's intentions and remotely view the outcome helps!

Just as in an army, the plan must be discussed by everyone involved. When the plan has been agreed, it is put to the staff, although it is made clear that the manager is in charge and responsible for the ultimate decision. Members of the staff are all shown their parts in the plan, and, once briefed, they run through what they have to do until they are certain about their roles. This makes them confident in performing their allotted tasks; they are more likely to implement the plans made by their managers and a positive cycle ensues. Pride in one's skills is itself a powerful motivator; training is not a luxury but a necessity for psiops management.

3. Command as service

The purpose of leaders is to enable people to do their work as well as possible. Staff need to satisfy the customers' needs; psiops managers serve their staff's needs. In the military world, it is the commander's duty to see that the troops are well equipped, trained and briefed. Every officer must look after his men. In the battle zone, the commander makes sure that his troops are properly billeted before going to sleep himself. When the battle begins, the commander does everything in his power to make sure that his troops have everything they need to win. Reading any of Tom Clancy's

US military history books gives one the feel of what I mean.

Likewise, psiops managers acknowledge that they are there to serve the needs of subordinates so that staff can get on with the job at hand. Psiops managers never rest until the 'troops' have whatever is needed to do the job. They persevere until the job is complete and the customers have been satisfied.

4. Command by leadership

Leaders are followed. People need them. Although leaders come in many shapes and sizes, everyone has some kind of mental picture of a leader. In order to command a group of people, the leader has a responsibility to conform to that picture. In military circles, the selection of leaders is carefully controlled. Would-be officers pass through stringent tests before they are accepted, and the training of officer cadets is designed to foster the quality of leadership. They are taught to become leaders so that their men will accept them as such.

But, as we have seen, to work successfully, hierarchical organisations need a free flow of feedback from below. In an army, one of the functions of the non-commissioned officers (NCOs) is to act as an information channel between the men in the ranks and the junior officers. A good NCO is invaluable; his experience and knowledge of the soldiers enables the newly-commissioned officer to avoid the worst effects of his faults and inexperience. SAS combat cadres are led by senior NCOs for this reason.

The psiops manager appreciates the need to be pigeon-holed as a leader in the minds of subordinates. Leaders fall into three classes:

a) The dashing, brave and gallant hero, who leads because those who follow have a wish to emulate his daring deeds.

b) The quietly competent leader; a master of planning who knows where to go and how to capitalise on situations. People are moved to follow by this leader's intelligence, insight and grasp of reality.

c) The master of reward, who motivates with success and riches.

A psiops manager realises that all three of these aspects of leadership are essential for acceptance as a commander. Psiops managers carefully tailor their image and activities so that they are pigeon-holed as leaders. RS is a vital key in the success of this endeavour.

The dashing hero always presents a brave face (even if scared rigid). The clothes, manner and speech of this leader are contrived to fit the mould. In the military world, badges, uniforms and insignia immediately proclaim who is the boss, and in business, too, managers must put on the appropriate uniform. In Britain, where accent has strong overtones of status, managers must sound authoritative but classless – otherwise they will not be taken seriously or will be resented.

Psiops managers build on their merits and makes sure that others appreciate what those merits are, though not in a cocky or aggressive way. The manager can work harder, better or have more knowledge than subordinates.

The manager must be self-critical. Weak points must be identified and eliminated, since these impair the manager's ability to lead. People put leaders on a pedestal, but at the same time much is expected from them, and if bosses are found wanting, the judgements can be ruthless.

The psiops manager rewards people who achieve and contribute to the organisation. The reward may be no more than a word of praise, or it may be something more tangible such as promotion, money or a better place to work.

Control

1. Control of events

In order to control, it is necessary to know what is happening. Remote viewing gives the commander this ability. It is then possible to shape events rather than just react to them. A good commander in the field attempts to draw the enemy into a particular course of action. Likewise, the psiops manager uses RV to bring goals to fruition. When staff are forced to react to crisis after crisis due to bad administration and unsympathetic management, morale is sapped and performance suffers.

2. Control for survival

When survival depends on an order being correctly executed, soldiers do not balk at following their officers. But in civilian organisations, immediate pressure is generally absent. A good manager will explain to staff exactly what is at stake. A psiops manager realises that people do not do things in a vacuum, and RS helps them to understand how their work fits into the goals of the organisation as a whole. Meme theory is vital in this context.

3. Control by hierarchy

In a military organisation, an order is given and carried out. The chain of command is strictly upheld and immediacy is built in. In commercial organisations, discipline is, of course, more lax. Committees of individuals come to mutual agreement or fall into warring camps. If such a thing happened in an army, it would be annihilated in battle; in the business world, events move more slowly but the end result is just the same.

In a civilian situation, it is necessary to adapt the military principle of hierarchical control to make it acceptable. The most important point to realise is that unless a command has a positive overtone embedded in it, it will be implemented slowly or wrongly. Thus, the psiops manager appreciates that immediacy can only come in a civilian organisation if success is injected into the activity and a positive feedback cycle is set up by using meme theory.

In the military, peer group pressure is important. Bad soldiers are constrained by their comrades. Likewise, in hard-working and productive staff cells, there are social pressures encouraging all to pull their weight. This is one reason why staff cells are so important; they promote group identity.

To maintain control, a psiops manager tries to adapt military principles of leadership where appropriate and use RV/RS to optimise this process.

4. Control: imparting fearlessness

The last aspect of control presents difficulties, since it runs counter to much current practice. Psiops managers, like their military counterparts, try to promote a fearless view of the world where subordinates are willing to embrace new methods of work. They also attempt to give job satisfaction to their staff: the sense that they are getting something positive out of their work as well as money. When staff are fearless and enjoy job satisfaction, they are productive. The problem is that they are also difficult to control. Poor managers in charge of such a body of individuals could find themselves in trouble, because these staff do not blindly follow orders.

The military have no choice but to take the risk, training elite forces with strong group identities, who know that they are doing a worthwhile job. Given an order to undertake a dangerous mission behind enemy lines, elite forces immediately apply all their energy to the task. The military have found that raising the self-esteem of its troops, banishing their fear through training and instilling pride in their competence makes them easier to control. The only trouble is that elite troops can pose a threat to a weak commander.

To return to the business world, to gain and keep control, managers must win respect. Employees will only pay lip service to a manager who they consider inferior and unwilling to accept good advice. In an army, newly commissioned young officers are indeed inferior in experience to the old war dogs under their command, but the culture allows for this; officers suffer no loss of face if they seek advice from their NCOs. Soldiers appreciate this, and are therefore willing to follow the raw officer. In effect, because the officer regards the NCO as a trusted advisor, the men are transferring their respect from their own NCOs to that officer. This can be seen as 'vertical feedback'. Understanding how to spread positive memes is vital in this context too.

In the commercial world, the equivalent of the NCO is the foreman or factory floor supervisor, but in many large organisations, the culture leaves no room for vertical feedback between the workers in overalls and those in suits. Psiops managers are not too proud to seek advice from their experienced staff and to let it be known that such advice will be accepted if it seems right. Command and the responsibility of making the final decision remains with the manager, but since those who are best at the job in hand have been closely involved, they never say that if they were in charge, they could have done better. The best have given their advice and it has been taken. Things can still go wrong, of course, but if they do, there will be no recriminations. Using remote viewing, the psiops manager can foresee problems and be in control at all times. RS shows her/him how to best implement actions with staff by getting into their mindset.

In some companies, pressure to cut costs has led to 'fear management'. Put plainly, this means 'do what you are told or lose your job'. This concept of control has existed since time immemorial, only it used to be your head that you'd lose!

In the short term, fear management is certainly effective, but it has a major drawback – no better way could be devised for initiating a destructive feedback cycle. The larger the organisation, the longer the destruction will take, but the outcome is always the same.

Psiops managers should avoid fear management like the plague. It works, but the price is high as it turns off positive memes. Good military forces like that of the US do not turn their soldiers into fear-wracked starvelings. Likewise, psiops managers do not frighten their staff with threats of unemployment, with the aim of turning them into wage-slaves afraid for their standard of living. Instead they stimulate staff to accept psiops management principles, which will give their company – and their own jobs – an excellent chance of survival in the chaotic 21st century.

Communication

Military forces depend upon communication. Psiops organisations and managers must realise that information transfer is of the utmost importance. Communication capability must be built into the organisation to enable it to run in real-time. Nowadays, satellite reconnaissance provides real-time information to military commanders. Likewise, in the business world, technology can be exploited to provide managers with real-time information about the organisation and its markets.

The difficulty with all this information is that managers can be overwhelmed; important information might be overlooked or ignored. A remote viewer is not so effected by adverse conditions. Psiops information theory dictates:

1. Personal contacts are as important as they always were. Military commanders mix with their men and know key personnel. Officers know the names of all the troops for whom they are responsible. Research has shown that people can only know about 150 people properly; when there are more, we merely pigeon-hole them. Armies are divided into units containing less than 150 so that everyone can know each other. The unit can then remain a cohesive whole. Psiops managers, too, know all the people under them, so that when they meet, there can be an exchange of social niceties. This social interaction blends the group together and promotes a positive feedback.

2. Vertical information and feedback channels are vital. We have already discussed the role of NCOs in passing on the views of the soldiers. Group remote viewing on company projects binds managers together to a common cause.

3. Horizontal channels for information transfer are also required. These are the management nodes – small groups of managers from different departments, who discuss anything of mutual interest. Then they can use remote viewing to see how it affects the future of the company. In military organisations, this function is performed by the officers' mess. In civilian organisations, sports clubs and canteens serve as important channels for information transfer.

4. Psiops information theory is applied to augment the capability of the company; the purpose is to order the enormous data flow passing through the organisation, to prevent it from taking on a life of its own and enable it to be used to promote success. Remote viewers can handle much more data and order it in a coherent way.

Communication in psiops organisations is such a big subject involving integrated RS and RV that, for the present, we have been able to do little more than hint at a few important points.

Intelligence

Intelligence is about gathering, processing, understanding and acting on information. Remote viewing and sensing are the best way for managers to find out what competitors are doing or to study competitors' research and forthcoming products. No secret is secret anymore with this technology.

1. Intelligence as information-gathering

Military organisations devote much time and money to gathering information about potential enemies. Governments would not spend vast sums of money on this if it did not bring benefits. All organisations should appreciate the power of intelligence. Remote viewing and sensing are the new weapon in this arsenal. Nothing is a secret to RV/RS. Satellite surveillance has provided military organisations with the technology to achieve real-time management in the battlefield. In civilian organisations, the marketplace is the equivalent of the war zone, and technology such as point-of-sale terminals has made it possible to maintain an up-to-date picture of customers' requirements. With remote viewing and sensing, all psiops managers can have their own personal psychic satellites to spy on competitors and even look into the future.

Inside the organisation, psiops managers take advantage of management nodes and horizontal and vertical management lines to pick up as much information as possible about the organisation and its environment. Like their military counterparts, they understand that information wins battles. To this end, psiops managers use remote viewing and sensing technology to learn:

a) How to increase their capacity for data-processing by scanning through printed material instead of reading it diligently word by word.

b) To conserve energy and increase their stamina.

c) To improve the quality of their thinking, to make the best of whatever information is available.

d) To extract from a mass of data the information they require, and to present it in goal-orientated form. To these ends they learn the following skills:
   i) Speed reading
   ii) Directed attention, to focus attention on a problem in a relaxed manner, and to conduct potentially tense transactions in a relaxed manner.
   iii) Visualisation in pictorial form on their mental cinema screen, to improve memory retrieval and data processing.

In a world where managers are bombarded with ever-increasing quantities of information, the individual's reaction can lead either to destructive feedback or positive feedback. To exploit information to establish a positive feedback cycle, never become submerged in minutiae; if you try to take in every last scrap of detail, you will quickly suffer from overload. Hone your awareness and then skim over information, trusting your instincts to alert you to anything of interest. The effectiveness of subliminal advertising demonstrates that messages are picked up when required. Managers can make use of this to bring the important information to conscious perception. In the process, the technique induces a positive feedback cycle, since it damps down the banal internal 'conversations' which are fed by concentrating on minor details.

2. Intelligence in action
Psiops managers try to realise their full potential. They know

that straining and stressing themselves and others is harmful. It uses energy and leads to unhappiness and ill health. Psiops managers therefore do everything they can to promote positive attitudes in themselves and others by using meme theory. Once established, memes are self-perpetuating and everybody in the organisation will be working to their full potential.

3. Intelligence in command

It has long been known that what counts is not just the command, but the tone of voice behind it. Uplifting speeches before the battle have long been the hallmark of the good commander. Psiops managers, too, understand that it is not enough just to know what to do. Others must somehow be persuaded to do it. Psiops managers must become masters at embedding positive overtones in all they say and do. They know that otherwise, there can be no positive feedback and no psiops managers. If managers cultivate themselves as centres of success, and radiate this feeling of self-worth and self-esteem, they will spur their people to achievements which they would never have imagined. Enter the mindset of your staff to know which buttons in their psyche to press for motivation.

4. Intelligence in relation to ideas

Psiops managers constantly reflect on their successes and failures and revise their ideas accordingly, by remote viewing virtual reality to optimise decision making – using future RV to see how it works beforehand.

Military organisations constantly upgrade the knowledge of senior officers through training programmes of various kinds, and good civilian organisations do likewise. As we have seen, resistance to change is a particular problem in civilian organisations, and psiops managers must understand how people work as groups, applying the principles of motivation and learning to hone the corporate culture, using remote viewing to see how best to go about this and RS to see what works with staff and management.

C3I in practice

The core competency involved in lean management, C3I, is essentially about upgrading the managers' skills to enable them to implement psiops management. But managers, arriving at their desks, find a stack of paper waiting to be dealt with. How are they to pick out what needs to be done?

Only three criteria need to be applied. Does it help to provide a product or service which a customer wants? Does it form part of a commitment to excellence? Does it lead to new and improved modes of working or is new and useful knowledge gained?

To understand what this means, let us consider the contents of a manager's in-tray. The paperwork can be divided into three categories:

1. Requests for you to do something – tasks to carry out or provide information or make payments to others.

2. Acknowledgements that you have done something – receipts, payments, delivery notes, information notes.

3. Noise.

To deal with this, there are two simple steps to follow:

Step one: Eliminate the noise.
Step two: Prioritise the others in order of urgency.

We term this just-in-time (JIT) management. If you go through the contents of your in-tray with only the above two points in mind, you will soon get the hang of this idea.

Having prioritised the tasks, the manager must now apply psiops management principles. To achieve this effectively, formal structures must be used intelligently, remembering that everyone is working for the same organisation and that experts in many fields are to be found in unexpected places. Most people these days have had several careers, and if you add in the knowledge acquired from leisure activities, there is a wealth of skill to draw upon. Normally this knowledge is bottled up, but someone in your company can help you get your job done better, and there are many people in your organisation that you could help. Value your network of informal contacts and use it whenever you need. Never forget to acknowledge that you have received their help, but do not push your own claims about what you have done.

Having called up all the help that you can lay your hands on by use of the psiops information network, the use of remote viewing and sensing, your activities are now directed towards the task at hand. What next? The world moves on. Keep ahead of the moves using remote viewing. Or do you think that you are too busy to psychically spy? Jobs for life are a thing of the distant past. Don't be surprised if you find yourself sidelined.

One of the purposes of JIT management is to provide you with the time to talk to other people and browse through the literature. Increase your knowledge of that which could be of value to you. Train and practise to broaden and deepen your skills. Evaluate new technology as it comes along and use it if it can help you do your work. Keep abreast of new developments. Be aware of what is happening in your industry as a whole and use remote viewing to see future developments in the industry.

At the very least, this will prevent your job from becoming tedious. You will be seen as competent and well-informed; in fact, you will be competent and well-informed. If the chop comes, you are less likely to be one of the victims, and head-hunters and promotion boards will view you favourably.

Summary

JIT management, used in conjunction with the psiops management network and remote viewing and sensing, gives you the time to get on with the job, and the opportunity to talk to other people and increase your knowledge and capabilities. This creates fertile ground for identifying microclimates of opportunity and exploiting them. The process feeds on itself and we see here yet another example of positive feedback.

NINE

ADVANCED REMOTE VIEWING
AND REMOTE SENSING

Advanced RS and RV protocols are needed to master psiops. I feature here the most advanced protocols ever published. This exercise requires you to complete the first 28 steps of the relaxation techniques described on pages 71–73. Then:

1. Intend your epicentre of awareness inside your thalamus, the limbic brain centre posited as the 'organ of attention': from there, intend the mental laser light of your DA to erase all preconceptions of the target site from your mental cinema screen which is used for RS. Scan your whole brain for preconceptions of the target site and intend your DA to erase all data connected with your RS target which does not pertain to the truth.

2. Call up your biophysical vehicle which will face you on your mental screen of DA. Command your DA to scan your biophysical RS vehicle and erase all false data about your target person.

3. Repeat the above programming stage, but take it a stage further and use your DA to scan your biophysical body. This time command your DA to erase all false data that

pertains to the totality of all the RS experiences you will ever attune to.

4. Begin to use your DA to reprogram your biophysical vehicle, to optimise its accuracy by augmenting the primary consciousness attributes your latent morpho-genetic-based RS vehicle consists of. Intend the primary consciousness programming to pass from your brain into your thalamus. From there, it needs to pass along the transmission line of your DA into the hara of your bio-physical vehicle, along the silver cord of energy that connects your RS vehicle with your physical body via the midsections of both bodies.

5. From the position of your biophysical vehicle, use DA on the brain using the remote influencing capabilities of your biophysical fields to change your own brain functioning for enhanced and more accurate RS. Concentrate on the following areas:
   a) Reprogramming the neural networks for optimum RS efficiency.
   b) Erasing mental blocks – normal human software that limits your efficiency.
   c) Inaccurate software that interferes with efficient tar-geting of the RS vehicle.
   d) Negative software that interferes with the accurate uptake of information from the biophysical vehicle while it is RS.
   e) Memes which are acting as mental viruses and drain-ing your adaptive energy.
   f) Memes that hold you in the consensual reality of normal people that limits your paranormal abilities,

gives you cancer, heart disease, mental illness and stress.

g) The memes you hold of reality which so limits you that you cannot reach your paranormal abilities.

h) Blocks that keep you from entering the mindset of your RS targets.

i) Knowledge that the mental model your RS target inhabits is not the same mental model as yourself. This is because as a remote sensor, you have changed the parodyne of the mental mindset (or mental grid, as Swann called it) you use to model reality. To interconnect with normal people, you have to appreciate that the memetic totality of the their mental software is a poor, twisted thing, compared to your own. You will have to build a special translation software meme to accurately upload information from their mental domain.

As a next exercise, practise scientific remote sensing (SRS) in which you RS a friend and photos he or she chooses to view RS, with immediate feedback on the accuracy of your sensing.

You will find as your RS vehicle raises its energy level and consciousness – from its latent morphogenetic state to primary consciousness (where it can be aware of its surroundings) on to high-order consciousness where you can be aware of yourself living in a biophysical vehicle – one can correlate increased accuracy of RS with this elevation in biophysical development. At first, 15 per cent accuracy is normal, and by the time you have high-order consciousness, 85 per cent or higher accuracy can be achieved, which will increase toward the theoretical limit of 100 per cent.

Rewriting the memes that inhabit your being may seem a trivial pursuit but the power they hold over you is immense and it holds you back from developing your paranormal potential. Worse still, the absolute belief people have in their false reality dampens down all paranormal activity that does not fit into their model of reality. In paranormal affairs the entity that has the most adaptive energy can control the entity with the lesser energy level. If we take the summation of humanity which has absolute belief in its false version of reality, then it can hold on to the conviction by using its immense adaptive energy level to block all paranormal activity. Geniuses such as Ingo Swann fought against this immense pull of the common consensus and practised RS regardless. He could do this because he effectively edited out all the negative memes he was carrying, which, combined with high natural psi abilities, was enough to pull him out of the false human reality. He could automatically remotely view unfettered from this human–created paranormal damping reality we call the real world.

Remote sensing of the group unconscious

The group unconscious is the sum total of the biophysical mindfields of humankind that reside on this planet.

As a first exercise, RS people's link with the group unconscious. You will find that everybody is intimately connected to the group unconscious. By this means, everyone is connected to everyone else. This offers ways of using one person to enter the mind map, and company mindset of an organisation that person belongs to.

RS a person who works for a large organisation. Using remote sensing, follow their link to the group unconscious and from there see how it branches to other members of the organisation. Ignore links which look the same as the person's, as these will be links to family members. Also ignore links that shine, as these will be links to friends and loved ones. Look for a large number of dark-looking links which bind that person to the workplace.

Follow these links into the person's organisation and begin to scan their workmates. Go upwards and let the links take you to the managing director or head of the organisation.

Project your biophysical RS vehicle into their brain, and start to upload images of what that organisation is doing and what its aims are. Look for black areas in their awareness that hide secrets they do not wish to divulge, and set your biophysical RV vehicle to upload all aspects of what you find interesting.

Next, follow the links this person has to other people in his clique, by accessing his or her link with the group unconscious. Using remote sensing, follow their link to the group unconscious and from there see how it branches to other members of the heads of that and other organisations. Again, ignore links which look the same as the person's and links that shine, as these will be links to friends and loved ones. Look for a large number of dark-looking links which bind that person to their power clique.

Follow these links into the minds of the heads of this and connected organisations and begin to scan their data stores. Go upwards and let the links take you to the head of that group of organisations.

Let your biophysical body access their brain and upload all the information you require. Remember, biophysical bodies are data carriers and can store vast amounts of information that you can later access using your brain. The speed of uptake of the biophysical fields is very fast, and that of the brain relatively slow, so it may take months for you to become fully aware of what information you have scanned from the heads of leading organisations.

In remote sensing, the need to remain in the theta state whilst carrying out RS means that advanced methodologies need to be used. Why is the theta state so important? Paranormal phenomena are very strong. They are extremely rare in the general population, so how could such a strong force like psi-fields (see glossary) be made so weak?

In modern society, the entire population has a defined view of what is real and what is not real. The summation of all their conscious intent is amplified by their group psi-fields, and the six billion people on the planet produce a very powerful psi-field that effectively banishes paranormal phenomena. This is the psi-damping-field that covers the planet and makes paranormal abilities so weak in RS operators who wish to use their talents. All six billion people have a summated biophysical field – the group conscious biophysical field that amplifies the consciousness of humanity with respect to making some phenomena possible and others impossible. This means that going down to the shops and buying a new outfit on your credit card is reality, while levitating up into the clouds is ferociously expunged by the power of the group consciousness's psi-damping-field. This PDF effectively ruins our health by making cancer possible and the self-psychic healing of our tumours improbable. Spontaneous remission of cancer does occur, but is unpredictable – like paranormal phenomena.

Theta and remote sensing

The theta state is important in that it allows the normal person imprisoned in consensual reality to escape the shackles of the so-called 'real world'. To do this, the PDF generated by small-minded humanity must be disrupted. In order to do this, the psi-operator must attune his biophysical body with the Earth's biophysical field. By this means, the much larger biophysical field of the Earth can erase the effects of the much smaller PDF generated by humanity. Theta is the gateway to the paranormal in that it allows the RS operator to resonate with the biophysical field of the planet. This boosts the biophysical field of the psi-operator to the extent that paranormal phenomena become possible. The Earth resonates with a frequency of about 7.82 HZ, called the Schumann Resonance – the natural frequency of the planet. Theta begins at this frequency, so RS at this frequency will allow RS to become possible. The biophysical field of the RS operator merges with that of the planet at the Schumann frequency and enables the RS operator to escape the effect of the PDF.

To enter this state it is even better if you are part of a group, as the summation of a group biophysical field occurs when RS is carried out in unison. The military groups in the US used the group effect to boost their RV. As an expert in the scientific study of biophysics, I have developed stratagems to dramatically boost the paranormal capabilities of RS operators.

Amplification of remote sensing and other paranormal abilities

Relax and visualise your thalamus. Intend your epicentre of consciousness, the 'I' part of your being to be in the thalamus. Control your directed attention and focus the beam of this mental laser on your reptilian brain, especially the *locus coeruleus*. Command the *locus coeruleus* to shut down, detonating the brain stress system. Reprogram the *locus coeruleus* to be totally goal-fixated on RS and to ignore all stressors unless they are actually life threatening.

Next, focus the mental laser of your DA on your limbic system, especially the hypothalamus, which you command to lower its neurochemical and electrical stimulation of your brain stress system so that you reach theta. Reprogram the hypothalamus to ignore all stressors unless they are actually life threatening.

Focus your DA on the limbic system which you need to command to ignore all stressors that are not life threatening. The goal is to inculcate a theta state in your waking state so that you can resonate in sympathy with the Schumann frequency of the Earth's biophysical field. In this way you can display paranormal abilities even when facing the withering blast of humanity's PDF. By constantly operating in the theta state the psi-operator becomes more and more detached from humanity's PDF and displays larger and larger psi-latency.

You should completely program your limbic system:

1. Reprogramme the thalamus to boost your attention and make it focus for DA.

2. Reprogramme the hypothalamus to lower your basal brain stress level to theta.

3. Reprogramme the hippocampus to boost all aspects of your memory, both short and long-term. This will

enhance uptake of data from your biophysical RS vehicle to boost RS, RS and RI.

4. Reprogram the amygdala – which is the pea-shaped brain centre in the limbic system associated with pleasure and pain responses – to activate your pleasure receptors every time you carry out RS, so that your limbic system is flooded with positive emotions every time you practise. Since the limbic system controls volitional decision-making in humans, this will mean that you will motivate yourself to carry out more and more RS the more you practise it. In time, you will so stimulate the limbic system that every time you use your senses, RS will be incorporated into your portfolio of senses. You will have developed a permanent sixth sense.

5. Next, reprogramme the reticulate gyrus (another limbic centre associated with cognitive fuctioning) to boost your RS capacity by boosting your capacity to process RS information.

6. See the limbic system as a totality and see all its connections with the cortex and hindbrain. Through these connections flood the rest of the brain with positive emotional stimuli via neurochemical transmitters and neuroelectrical signals to the point that the whole of your brain experiences an orgasmic-like trance condition every time you practise RS.

    By these means the brain can be driven into lower levels of delta that enable you to link into deeper and deeper shells of the Earth's biophysical fields. In this way you can reach the elevated trance-like state of the yogic master who has augmented control over his body and the world around him or herself.

7. Let your DA travel to your pituitary gland and command this gland to shut down the stress-hormones that keep your brain and body in a heightened state of anxiety all through the day.

8. Reprogramme your cortex to run RS simulations and processing of enormous complexity. Open up all areas of your cortex to boost your data processing capacities to the tesla-level (see glossary), where you can visualise complete scenarios in your brain. By doing this you are setting your RS capabilities to include reading minds and accessing the complex data contained therein.

9. Return to your pituitary and command your gland to shut down the brain stress system every time your cortex runs RS simulations or data processing. Use DA on the limbic system to flood your brain with pleasur-able emotions every time you use enhanced cortex capabilities to produce a positive feedback cycle (to make this cortex enhancement permanent).

10. Return to the pituitary and follow the hormonal path-ways to the adrenal glands atop the kidneys. Command your adrenal glands to shut down the fight-or-flight hormonal response system and to boost the feedback to shut down the brain stress system. Command the whole hormonal system to shut down the brain stress system response the more your limbic system is flooded

with positive responses by use of RS, RI and RV. By this means, a very powerful feedback system is set up that lowers your body's stress levels every time you use RS.

11. Return your DA to your reptilian brain and command your biophysical RS vehicle to take control of this brain stress system detonator so that no matter what stressors you are subjected to, you never lose your link with your biophysical vehicle. So even though you may be under enormous stressor levels, you will not display high brainwave activities because your bio-physical vehicle has taken command of your brain stress system.

Self-healing

This whole reprogramming of your brain is necessary if you are to ever emulate the handful of high-order psi-operators in existence. If you wish to carry out self-healing you must also reach this level of proficiency. This is because the PDF generated by humanity switches on oncogenes in the general population, and elevates the brain stress system to insane levels; it also damages the telomeres (see glossary) causing premature ageing, genetic cell damage and errors in replication. The PDF is composed of the totality of human morphogenetic fields which have field-matched and coa-lesced into a gigantic high-order biophysical artificial intelligence. This field not only controls what is possible and what is not but blocks all entry into paranormal reality and uses its morphogenetic nature to make possible genetic illness and the concomitant damage that this does to us: cancer, accelerated ageing, fragility to pathogens and stressors. One can see that the PDF concept takes us much farther down the road of suffering the human condition than we need suffer if the human PDF did not exist. Since the psi-field phenomena are the strongest of all the forces available to man, the unconscious melding of all our morphogenetic fields (see glossary) into one colossal summation of all our biophysical fields defines and reinforces the human condition. Since almost all of us believe cancer is a dreaded killer and paranormal healing does not exist, we weaken our own immune systems to the extent that they only display a fraction of their true potential.

Once you are in the theta state, the Earth's biophysical field swamps out the human PDF and enables your body to cure itself of damage that would kill a normal person. It also enables you to absently heal anyone you wish.

By practising biophysical RS technology, the knock-on effect is huge, boosting longevity and resistance to disease. This primarily occurs because the psi-operator frees her/himself from the evil intents of the human PDF biophysical AI that causes untrained people to age at a vastly accelerated rate, blocks all their paranormal abilities, and makes them totally vulnerable to disease, as well as causing mental illness.

Advanced remote viewing and the future

For looking into the future with RV, the area of the brain which enables precognition is a little understood area. US experiments in showing people pornographic photographs which are present in a larger pack of non-emotive pictures – such as those of the countryside – has shown an elevation in physical responses five seconds before the pornographic photo was observed. This indicates that at a deep subconscious level, precognition of emotive events occurs. This would have high survival value, as the ability to know of danger in the future would allow it to be avoided. Precognition, if it is carried by psi-genes, would therefore be reinforced by natural selection. Those who could see into the future and avoid danger would be more likely to live on and have children.

In combat, this 'sixth sense' of danger is heightened. Vietnam veterans had numerous paranormal experiences, such as RV of mines, bullets being seen in flight and Vietcong traps being psychically sensed. A famous example is of a US soldier spotting a Vietcong soldier with grenades hidden on his torso, disguised as a peasant by the roadside. Fighter pilots have to develop a sixth sense which is called situational awareness; a brain state where both hemispheres of the brain are working equally and in synchrony. An almost Zen-like state, where there is no chaos in one's thinking and everything seems more real. Situational awareness involves instinctively taking in a wealth of information, evaluating it, and reacting correctly with a panoramic view of everything around the pilot, in his or her mind's eye. American fighter pilots call it 'having the clue' – a state where they can fly their plane and have full visuo–spatial awareness.

If both hemispheres of the brain in synchrony bring about almost precognitive vision around the fighter aircraft, this points to brain centre balancing being a key aspect of looking into the future. When the remote viewer enters the theta state, this balancing of brain hemispheres naturally takes place.

Theta brain rhythms also enable more of the information we receive from the biophysical body to be left unmolested.

As we have seen, 90 per cent of the information we receive is filtered out by the thalamus (the limbic system of the brain). Neurophysiologist Karl Pribram of Stanford University, California, describes this perceptive filtering as the Bowery Effect. The Bowery was an elevated railroad in New York that was demolished. After the late night service ended the police were inundated with phone calls about something strange happening at exactly the time the train would normally pass through that neighbourhood. This went on for months after the railway had gone. People were subconsciously picking up on the lack of noise at the time they were expecting the train and panicking because they did not hear the train passing. Consciously they thought something was wrong, so they phoned the police.

Information is normally filtered out by the limbic system. It is then run through the software we use to tailor the world to a preconceived reality. This is a product of memes given to us by parents and peer groups throughout our lives. Theta enables us to unblock these mental filters that blinker us to RV and other paranormal phenomena.

For precognitive RV, we have to look at how the brain hemispheres process information and how this may have a bearing on psychically looking into the future. The bio-physical body can travel through time, as it is not limited by the three dimensions of space and one of time that our physical body is constrained by. The left hemisphere of the brain deals with linear data and thoughts. It is a linear processor, plodding from a to b to c.

The right hemisphere deals with lateral, non-linear thought processes. It carries out parallel processing, for example: a to z to b to y, in the human mind's eye.

Remotely viewing the future appears to come from the

left-hand side of the perceptual picture, while remote viewing the past appears to come from the right-hand side of our perception. The fact that the left-hand field of our perception is connected with future events and that the right-hand field is concerned with past events can be explained by the different activities each hemisphere of the brain undertakes. The right side of the brain controls the left side of the body and, since this part of the brain can handle parallel processing, it finds it easy to run probabilistic non-linear thought, which is used for thinking about the future. The many variable probabilistic simulations we run to forecast the future of our actions is also used for looking into the future using RV.

The left hemisphere of the brain is a linear processor so it handles data in the a-b-c-d-e- fashion. It deals with known variables and data. It therefore runs memories and simulations of past events to match present events, which it then reruns to conform to past mental programmes. Since it controls the right side of the body, due to the hardwiring in the brain, past images appear on the right side of our mind's eye. Left-handed people have brain hemispheres which work in the opposite manner.

When the left and right hemispheres are working in synchrony, then the person experiences situational awareness, as described above.

When RV the future, the right side of the brain deals with the information being given to it by the biophysical body. The theta brain state enables situational awareness, where the information can be quickly passed between right and left hemispheres for evaluation. Theta consciousness enables right-hand dominant brain action such as dreaming to take place and therefore is the perfect state for RV and precognitive RV.

Follow the instructions on pages 71-73, and after step 31:

32. Visualise your biophysical body travelling down a long corridor of light. As you get further from your physical body you should visualise the corridor of light branching left or right. To travel into the future take the left-hand branch and move along this corridor of light. The past is the right-hand branch. For short journeys into the future move your biophysical body only a short distance along this right-hand corridor, for long journeys move your biophysical body a large distance. Whatever distance you travel into the future to enter that time, open up a door in the corridor to step into that time. Once you are there, concentrate on any images you get and then fix your attention on the details you wish to remotely view. I like stealing theoretical physics from the future so I visit universities, secret military research labs and physics facilities, scanning the humans I encounter for information. By this means one can begin the arduous job of getting up to speed on future advancements. However, one needs to be trained to understand the science, and for a business person, looking for future products and innovations may be better. Whatever your speciality, this form of RV enables quantum leaps in development for the business using it. In the stock market, micro jumps into the future can enable the trader to increase his profits. Since 15 per cent efficiency was avowed by the CIA publicly for RV, and world experts such as McMoneagle and Moorhouse espouse 50–80 per cent accuracy, the bonus of the psiops-trained trader should increase within these parameters. Since I am not a mil-

itary trained remote viewer, but rather a remote sensor who derived his training from healing, I prefer to scan the minds of people in the future who have the knowledge I require. By leapfrogging a decade at a time one can keep up with developments into the far future. I have found this knowledge invaluable – I hope you too find what you are looking for by using future RV.

In this section you have come across a whole new way of working with RS and RV in the memetic mode, and for time travel. The aim has been to teach you how to optimise your RS and RV so that you can apply this expertise to your business. Continual repetition of this material is needed until you become comfortable with it. Once this happens and you apply it rigorously, not only will you achieve your psiops goals, you will feel marvellous as well, being the person you always wanted to be.

Psiops applications: psiops management theory

Modern management theory might be thought of as a collection of ideas developed over the past century. Part of it comes from the theory of military organisations, and the subject developed in response to the requirements of the needs of the large scale manufacturing industry.

A hundred years ago there was much faith in science and technology. People thought that nature was as predictable as a clock. And so a mechanistic view was built into the foundations of management theory. One of the attractions of a mechanistic theory is that it allows confident forecasting. One of the assumptions behind mechanistic theories is the idea of perfect rationality. But as we have seen, humans enjoy a rationality deficit – we are not mechanistic. Management could get by with mechanistic theories only because the world before 1960 was relatively stable. After that, things began to unravel. Naturally, there is a desire to cling to habits of thought that posit a stable world, but they can no longer deliver the goods.

Psiops management is an idea which has been borrowed partly from military theory, including paranormal warfare practices, although elements such as real-time management have been applied in industry for several years in areas such as process control. Real-time management was the only essential difference between the Gulf War and the Second World War. In the Gulf War, the US command knew exactly how the Iraqis had disposed themselves within the previous few hours and could tailor their responses accordingly. In the Second World War, commanders were constantly having to second-guess how the opposition would move and the result was often in the lap of the gods; the D-day landings were a close-run thing.

In the present-day business world, psiops management of situations seems to be a way of negotiating the problems and taking advantage of microclimates of opportunity as they present themselves by using remote viewing. In previous chapters we have looked at human performance and its relation to the group. We must now move up a level, and consider the formal structure of the organisation and how it can be tuned to achieve psiops management.

Psiops management structure does not disrupt the organisational structure and hierarchy already in place – it augments that structure. Established pecking orders are not disturbed and no departmental heads are liable to take offence – disastrous since their negative reaction would be counter-productive.

The psiops management structure resembles the pyramid depicted on a US dollar bill. It might be useful to link these in your mind's eye, to associate the organisational structure with wealth, success and all that goes with it! If you think that this idea too far-fetched, remember what we said about the principles of success – staff and managers in the organisation will immediately link psiops management with embedded overtones of success. It is important to forge this particular link, because injecting 'success' into all our ventures at the outset is helpful in motivating and bringing about the desired successful result. And keep thinking about that dollar bill – we shall be referring to it again later in this chapter.

The pyramid on our dollar bill has lost its apex. Where the top ought to be there is an all-seeing eye. A psiops management structure is exactly the same. The eye represents the top executives who can remotely view and sense, observing what is happening all around and below. The first four principles of psiops management structure relate to the aims and purpose of the top executives.

The principles of psiops management

Here is the first principle of psiops management:

Top executives look at everything that has a bearing on their organisation using RV and RS, keeping the whole company and its situation in mind. Top executives are bombarded with vast amounts of information. This can lead to 'data overload', stress and consequent bad decisions. But data processing must be regarded as the chief core competency of top executives. Psiops increases data-processing abilities by reducing stress and filtering out information which does not matter.

Strategic planning without psiops is fraught with insoluble

problems – who could have forecasted 9/11 and its effects on the US economy? The CIA could not, as they had given up remote viewing. After 9/11 they began a new RV project to spot terrorist attacks. Unfortunately, it is the job of top executives to look into the future and devise long-term projects. Since the future can develop in so many alternative possible ways, top management must recognise that by the time a long-term project is complete – five to ten years from its inception – the world may be very different from what was anticipated, and the investment could be wasted. To avoid this, psiops management theory advocates an approach which accepts that the future is very difficult to predict unless one uses remote viewing.

This gives us the second principle of psiops management: **Adaptive Strategic Planning**. Use remote viewing to:

1. Consider whether the project is likely to be profitable in the worst case scenario. If the potential profitability is very sensitive to variations in market and other conditions, the project must be regarded as high risk. Such a project is best left to companies which can tolerate losing large sums of money if things go wrong.

2. It is essential to build adaptability into any long-term projects to which the company commits itself. This is the cornerstone of the principle of project management known as Adaptive Strategic Planning (ASP).

3. ASP provides capacity within the investment for evolution to take advantage of even the worst conditions. It gives stability to long-term projects.

4. ASP also gives projects the flexibility which enables them to take advantage of MCOs.

5. Remote viewing enables executives to look into the future and to see how their new project fairs as they go through the processes mentioned above.

This brings us to the third principle of psiops management: **top executives constantly use their extensive knowledge to seek out MCOs**. They do this by using future RV to find products, innovations and new technologies from the future, and then marketing what they find of profit.

The fourth principle of psiops management: **accurate tactical planning**. Reducing the reaction time of an organisation by the use of psiops leads to improved short-term tactical planning. This is because in 'normal' organisations it takes many years to change attitudes and working practices. Top executives must therefore wait for many years to pass before it is possible to see if changes are successful. In a psiops organisation, reaction times – and hence implementation times – gradually fall to a matter of months. Thus top executives can quickly see whether a change is working. This is done by observing RS staff's reactions to change, and tailoring the change to boost the employees' self-importance, thus turning the reptilian complex off and lowering basal stress levels – the feel good factor for change.

If the above principles are ignored, things can go badly wrong. An example is the case of a refinery built by a major multinational oil company. Seven years into the project, the organisation reversed its strategy, and with it many other aspects of its operations. The senior middle managers were 'yes men' who immediately tried to implement this reverse doctrine. Staff were disgruntled. The end product was a refinery in which many of the crucial design factors were wrong; after more than a billion dollars had been spent, and two years after completion, production was only 20 per cent of planned capacity. As things turn out, this did not matter very much; the market for refined oil products had fallen to such an extent that the refinery would have been an expensive white elephant even if its performance had been 100 per cent.

Psiops structure in middle management

The task of top executives is to transcend the limited perceptions of company culture and take an overall view of the organisation and the world in which it operates. Remote viewing and sensing gives them this view. We now look at the next level of psiops management and enter the realm of organisational management.

The fifth rule of psiops management is to **augment the effectiveness of management by reducing the number of levels within the organisation to the optimum of three**: top executives, organisational management, and staff. But, as we have seen, upheavals are always harmful. Collapsing a company into just three levels of hierarchy would do more harm than good, since managers do not take kindly to being stripped of their importance – it promotes resistance and negative attitudes.

Memes seeded into the company to facilitate this structure are vital, these are given later.

In psiops structure, we use a three-level notional structure, but allow departmental heads and managers to retain their importance within the hierarchy. This is done by assigning the existing hierarchy to the truncated three-level management structure. As we have seen, hierarchy is helpful in establishing the positive feedback cycle, but if it is not to stifle initiative, information must be able to flow freely upwards from the bottom of the hierarchy, and horizontally across the hierarchy.

In the middle level of operational management, we introduce 'horizontal management networking'. Departments retain their importance, but this middle management level now sees itself as a unit. Instead of seeing themselves as rulers of antagonistic, competing departments, these networked managers are now encouraged to work in close conjunction, having regular communication on a personal basis. Thus, even though departmental heads still retain control within their spheres of influence, their ideas and views are passed on to other departments via 'management nodes' – small groups of managers who meet regularly on a formal basis. Rotating chairmanship of these nodes regularly between the mangers integrates their function.

The main functions of mangement nodes are as follows:

- They promote cohesiveness within the organisation by building group memes focused on RV/RS projects, both activities being amplified by group practise.

- They allow psiops information to pass through the organisation more quickly, reducing company reaction time.

- Regular meetings of management nodes promote order within the organisation, and constructive routines of this kind promote the positive feedback cycle by giving a sense of security. The group also amplifies all RV and RS activity the company is involved with, such as future technology RV.

- Social order within an organisation essential for psiops is facilitated. Meeting fellow-managers reinforces social bonding and provides an opportunity for gossip, which is an important social 'cement'. The theta state induced by psiops spreads through the node.

- They are a means of transmitting new information and new perspectives from other people and other departments. Regular meetings designed to implement psiops will discuss microclimates of opportunity (MCOs) which have been remotely viewed. Management node meetings provide the ideal framework for brainstorming sessions on MCOs and exploring how they might work.

This gives us the sixth rule of psiops structure: **managers from different departments should meet once a week or once a fortnight, to exchange information, work on projects and reinforce the psiops training process via management nodes**. These management nodes are networked to provide horizontal connections within the company, so that the lines of communication at the organisational management level of the hierarchy are as good as the vertical communications within departments. In the psiops management structure, these are called 'horizontal management lines'. We might here take another look at our dollar bill, this time at the right-hand side on the back, where the words *E pluribus unum* can be seen – from many, one. This is what horizontal management networking is all about. Having managers remotely viewing and sensing common interest events has this effect.

In a psiops organisation, the managers devote more time to remote viewing and sensing of future technology as this strengthens the core competency of the company. Finding and exploiting MCOs is a good example of this. To free the managers, enabling them to realise their full creative potential, psiops effectively re-engineers the managers' functions. It does not change their roles, but augments them. Useless tedious tasks are eliminated and their time and energy can be applied to goal-oriented pursuits that best utilise their professional abilities.

This gives us the seventh principle of psiops management structure: **efficiency requires lean management**. This implies a departure from the command-and-control philosophy to one which is knowledge-based and uses psiops. This knowledge is applied in two ways: to serve staff in their own particular modes of operation, and to enable them to do their work better.

Before they can do this, managers must be freed from the drudgery of having to continually check up on staff, who, in turn, are always asking their managers what to do.

This gives us the eighth rule of psiops management structure: **autonomous action**. Give staff the responsibility to carry out their work, doing it as they see fit, as long as they achieve what is required. Autonomous action helps to promote the positive feedback cycle as staff feel that they are being given responsibility, which boosts their self-esteem and motivation.

The ninth rule of psiops management structure is to **group staff in units of optimal size**. These are called staff cells, and allow staff with leadership quality to interact with staff who are happier if they are led. This promotes team spirit. Four is the optimum number per cell.

The tenth rule of psiops management structure is to **subdivide the organisation into units of not more than about 150 staff**. This is called the 'supercell', and will contain within it a number of staff cells.

In the eleventh rule of psiops management, we **deal with those activities in the organisation which might be termed 'self replicating'**. These are the repetitive activities on which staff are actually engaged for most of the time: running machinery, driving vehicles, processing paperwork and serving customers. If we can show staff how to do these as well as possible, using their own initiative as far as possible, they become locked into a positive feedback cycle which feeds on this success. These benefits are self-replicating, because the improved practices are picked up by others in the staff cell, exactly like a virus or meme. We call this 'the meme viruses of good practice'. There is no end to the benefits which can flow from this approach. Individuals grow in self-esteem when they know that they are doing their job well, and this feeling is reinforced in the group context. A good example of this can be seen in a well-run army platoon, under the charge of an experienced, competent NCO.

The twelfth rule of psiops management structure is to **recognise that information is the lifeblood of the organisation**, and that therefore the ability to remotely view and sense is invaluable to top companies. If staff and managers are relaxed, sociable and committed to their work, they will talk freely to each other about what they are doing and psiops information will be spread freely and quickly throughout the organisation. This will not happen in an organisation where staff are surly and managers constantly on the defensive.

The thirteenth rule of psiops management structure is to **network the organisation as a whole in the same way as management has been networked**. It is evident that the more that each part of the organisation sees itself as part of a team by mutual use of RS/RV, the more efficient the company will become. The alternative, found in poor organisations, is to have islands of activity separated by groups or individuals attempting to protect their realms.

This gives us the fourteenth rule of psiops management structure: **get everyone in the organisation to think of themselves as directing their many and varied talents, united to a common purpose**. See the company culture with positive memes. Staff and managers who feel that they *are* the organisation – and not mere wage slaves or yes-men – will perform better as they have unity through the organisation. The underlying principle of motivation – purpose – lies at the heart of this; common purpose must be regarded as one of the intangible but essential core competencies of any organisation.

The fifteenth rule of psiops management structure links up with the principle of adaptive strategic planning and is called **organisational evolution**. As we have seen, forecasts are unreliable unless we are remote viewers. We need to be adaptable, not just in the long term planning of projects, but in the organisation as a whole. The company should be able to evolve quickly and easily. Building in this evolutionary ability is essential in these fluid times. Remote viewing enables the business to foresee new 9/11s: suitcase nukes, or smallpox attacks for example. Try running a normal business without RV in the decades of unconventional war to come.

This brings us to the sixteenth rule of psiops management structure. In every organisation there is a bottleneck which fixes the rate at which a company can react. Find how to eliminate this bottleneck by remote viewing and sensing, as doing this will have a profound effect. The process can then be continued: **use remote viewing and sensing to find the next bottleneck**, get rid of it, and repeat until reaction time has been optimised. Psiops will then have been achieved.

The seventeenth rule of psiops structure is **optimise rather than change**. Optimisation will have a dramatic effect on the organisation without causing disruption. Change radically only that which must be discarded. RV of future technology allows the company to be ahead of all its competitors and under these conditions staff see optimisation as making money from these new technologies which come ready packaged and bug-free to their psiops managers.

An example of optimisation is RV benchmarking. Look at the best of the competition, then use future RV to beat its strong points and eliminate your own weaknesses.

As you can see, all the rules mesh together. They will enhance the power of the organisation so much that the talents and enthusiasm of managers and staff can flower. Most people have a vision of what it might be 'if only'; remote viewing sets the organisation on the path from 'if only' to 'has now become'. The remote viewing vision becomes reality. RS makes sure it is correctly implemented.

Information theory in psiops management

Managers can become isolated; rulers who have become remote from their subjects recur throughout history: Marie Antoinette is probably the most famous example.

Isolation can only be broken if there is a free and ample flow of information within the organisation. The trouble is that the information is corrupted at every stage. Managers can be yes-men to their superiors and autocratic in their attitude to those beneath. Staff can be resentful and may be in the habit of saying one thing and doing another. Everyone is busy telling others what they think they want to hear. Information transmitted in such circumstances is not to be relied upon.

How can information be transmitted reliably?

1. Using RV and RS protocols:
   a) Psiops protocols establish clearly laid down methods of passing on information. Passing between the sender (a disgruntled staff member who sees the business going wrong) and recipient (psiops manager) are a set of signals which say:
      i) (sender)   I am trying to contact you but I can't get through the organisational crap!

ii) (recipient)   I am ready to receive your message by RS.

iii) (sender)   ESP Message.

iv) (sender)   ESP Message ended.

v) (recipient)   Message received by RS.

Psiops managers should regularly scan for disgruntled staff as they generally have a message about organisational inefficiency that needs rectifying, masked from the manager by ass-kissers.

b) Organise the psiops information systematically and concisely. If the important data is embedded in a mass of superfluous material, it is likely to be overlooked. Concise information can be easily duplicated, reread, etc. and mistakes are less likely to creep in. The good thing about RS is that our biophysical body is a quantum computer and can filter out all garbage if ordered to while scanning. For this reason I almost never scan the minds of people for dialogue, but use the summated data fed to me by my biophysical body as it is the information I want – free from superfluous rubbish.

2. Use more than one channel of communication – use RS. A good example is looking at someone whilst they are talking. In a noisy room, it is often possible to make out what people are saying by watching their lips. Make sure, therefore, that information is passed through as many alternative channels as possible. If the message on one channel is corrupted, the correct message can be recovered on the alternative channel. Using RS to scan people's minds avoids this problem.

a) Use visual aids, written notes and practical demonstrations where appropriate to pass on the same information, as your audience are not remote sensors.

b) Confirm verbal messages in writing.

c) Have alternative routes, such as RS, for feedback from customers and staff, to make sure that you receive the real message.

d) Get to know the people you are communicating with and build up a rapport; devote some time initially to social topics such as family, car, sport, hobbies – subjects of mutual interest. Treat them properly and make them feel at ease. Impart a positive emotional overtone that will colour their recollection of that conversation. Use RS to see what is really on their minds, and empathic awareness to massage their feelings.

3. Information should be concise and to the point. Don't beat about the bush. Use data-filtered RS where your biophysical body filters out irrelevant information.

4. Cut down the number of times the message must be relayed from initiator to final recipient.

5. Check your RS to see whether it is true, to hone your abilities and confidence. Do this through:

a) Read-back. If you give someone a message, ask them what they think about it. If you give someone a complicated set of instructions, get them to explain in their own words what you have asked them to do; this, must, of course, be done with the utmost tact.

b) Cross-referencing. Try to obtain information on the same topic from different sources; if there is a contradiction, you can assume that some of the data is not to be relied upon. RS helps this process.

6. Filtering: make sure that personnel are not sent information which they do not require. Separate the important material from the junk.

   Because some junk is bound to get through, train yourself and your staff to extract it promptly and set it aside. The same should be done with RS, by training the biophysical body to filter out junk information.

7. Through networks: the information flow network should not correspond with the hierarchical structure of the organisation. Everyone should be able to communicate with everyone else. This idea is controversial, since managers do not like subordinates going behind their backs to top executives. It is up to the manager to secure the confidence of staff to ensure that this does not happen. RS enables this without human friction.

8. Information should be separated out into discrete and readily identifiable packages. Do this for all RS by training the biophysical body for this.

9. Make sure that information reaches the recipients at the right time: if it is received too late, it is useless; if too soon, it is liable to be forgotten by the time it becomes relevant. RI information into people's minds – SMA (the Supplementary Motor Area) facilitates this process.

Psiops information networks

Having looked at psiops information theory, let us continue

by seeing how it applies to the whole organisation.

Top executives need information and data augmented by RV/RS on three main topics:

1. How the world situation is affecting the company and its future.

2. How the company lies in relation to its competitors.

3. What is really happening in the company.

RV enables them to get the bird's eye view of the above. RS enables them to find any secret and hidden factor from the minds of people involved in the above list.

As we have seen, people do not see things as they really are, but the closer their picture comes to reality, the better the judgements that can be made. Unfortunately, seeing the world as it really is involves recognising unpalatable truths, but this is what top executives are paid for. To do this, they must free themselves of many preconceptions and learn remote viewing or use remote viewers.

A lot of accurate and up-to-date information is required. The organisation must hone its information-gathering abilities, and remote viewing enables a company to find out any secrets it wishes. All relevant journals, papers and other documents should be read and appraised. This may be time-consuming – 'you might not know what you are looking for until you have found it' – but regular scanning of publications gives information about markets, competitors and potential and microclimates of opportunity. Remote viewing enables these MCOs to be studied in a psychic virtual reality. In-house analysts are also helpful as they can quickly convert raw data into usable information. Networks of RV management nodes as well as contacts outside the company also enable top executives to keep their finger on what is going on, and market research departments would take the widest possible view. Future RV of technology to come is the ace in the hole for the psiops company as it enables them to keep ahead of all opposition.

These RV/RS augmented practices help top management to get an accurate view of the 'landscape around the company'. Once this is done, top management need to know how their own company is working. RS enables this. Once they know what their organisation is really like, top management can fine-tune it, getting departments and or divisions working as well as possible. The crucial factor is getting accurate information about the company. In some organisations there are problems:

1. Senior middle management is fixed in the 'yes sir' attitude, simply telling top executives what they think they ought to.

2. Junior management cover up their inexperience by doing the same thing.

3. Staff agree to do what supervisors and managers tell them, but actually do as they please.

4. Supervisors do not tell managers the real situation as it casts them in a bad light.

The net effect is that top management see a picture of their company which has been filtered through company culture.

Psiops management information systems using remote viewing and sensing bypasses these filters, take this negative filtering effect into account and erase its excesses. Management nodes would bring managers of roughly equivalent level together with the responsibility of implementing psiops in the organisation. If top executives were to ask them to give an accurate appraisal of the organisation, then the management node as a whole reports back and individual department heads would be less likely to be blamed for failure or paint their department in a rosy light. The interactions between departments could also be seen more accurately. Information from management nodes would therefore be less corrupted than that via normal channels. These management nodes can also work on future RV for technological appropriation of products the company may need, but cannot afford to design – as well as the technology not perfected yet.

As mentioned previously, junior managers copy their seniors' memes. Management nodes that incorporate junior managers would yield the same advantages to middle managers as the higher level management nodes would give to top executives.

Let us turn now to the staff. Team working promotes confidence and a sense of self-esteem, and peer pressure within staff cells will also help poorer staff members to increase their performance to live up to the group ideal by infecting them with positive memes. A group of people will feel better able to tell managers what is really going on. Individuals, on their own, do not usually like to speak for fear of being labelled 'difficult'. It is vital that everyone in an organisation should be given the opportunity to provide vertical information feedback, otherwise the situation in the 'trenches' is never really appreciated by top executives (unless they can RS). Executives who can remotely sense bypass this problem. This would help to combat the intractable problems that we outlined previously, promoting a company culture where reliable information was getting through. Top executives would be able to see both the company and its external environment in a truer perspective by using remote viewing and sensing.

Turning to customers or clients – psiops information systems allow the organisation to react more quickly to the customers' needs. Sales staff have better lines of communication to top executives, who have their finger on the pulse of customers, through the sales force and RS.

Contributory factors are:

1. RV of new point of sales technology.

2. Vertical and horizontal lines of communication built into the organisation, to provide prompt feedback on customers' needs. Interdepartmental team RV of future technology by management nodes cuts down on bottlenecks in new product development, because information and expertise of new technology is shared. This avoids snarl-ups due to one department not knowing the limitations of another.

3. Autonomous action by sales staff. This enables customers' needs to be met swiftly, as they do not need to pass all decisions up the line, with the resultant delays.

Embedding positive overtones and memes in information becomes habitual in the psiops organisation. People feed on meme information. But look at the situation in some organisations: information is passed around, but with memes of fear and anxiety embedded as an overtone. Prime examples of this are organisations dominated by fear management, where the 'knives are out'. You will no doubt have come across them.

People avoid things that make them feel bad. Memes carrying information that makes staff and managers depressed will be poorly remembered and acted upon. The problem is not so much the content of the information as the background it was associated with. An organisation dominated by a mood of alarm and despondency will embed these feelings in its staff and customers. Conversely an organisation that follows psiops management principles will embed memes with positive overtones in all information passing through the people who work for it. Staff and managers will only give their best if the job is a vocation rather than wage slavery. Making people feel good by use of positive memes when they transfer information, a company culture that gossips about good things going on in the company and staff and managers who associate work with success will all promote job satisfaction and self-esteem. This is not to advocate living in a fools' paradise where bad news is ignored. RS enables the psiops manager to know how to implement the above by pushing the right mental buttons in people's psyches.

People will filter out negative gossip and harbingers of alarm and despondency as it does not fit in with their picture of success. Performance is higher in organisations that believe in themselves and promulgate positive images of their activities. Future RV can make psiops companies a total success.

Psiops information networks

To conclude, let us look at ways psiops information net-works can facilitate positive meme transfer and uptake in the organisation:

- Strategic planning, as we have seen, is based on the false premise that future events can be predicted in detail. A psiops organisation seeks out knowledge from a variety of fields but uses remote viewing to find out what is impossible to know by other means. Tunnel vision is avoided. This is because ideas may come from many areas. More practicable and usable strategic planning is based on finding microclimates of opportunity by using remote viewing. Psiops information systems based on remote viewing enable senior managers to get the ordered data they need to guide the company from one short-term goal to the next.

- Long-term commitments or projects cannot always be avoided. Information is therefore required on ways of modifying long-term projects so they can adapt to change. Remote viewing is the perfect tool in this context. Large plants are difficult to design with adapt-ability in mind, but fortunately, new technology offers many ways to add this capability to projects. Psiops information systems should be designed to scour the rel-evant literature for ideas, then use future RV to find the solution – or something much better. Building in adapt-ability to plans is a microclimate of opportunity and could even become a core competency for the company that excels in this area. These adaptive long-term proj-ects should be the only ones psiops organisations undertake because of the unstable world situation. Use remote viewing to study their future.

- Procurement has been dominated by just-in-time buying. A good information system is a prerequisite, as materials are only ordered when they are needed. Stock is kept to the absolute minimum to cut costs. But the use of psiops information systems using remote viewing adds extra capability to procurement. It may be beneficial to stockpile scarce materials. JIT can lay a company open to not being able to fulfil an order and it can be detrimental to quality. JIT is fine as long as components or materials are easily obtained. More exacting components may be best stockpiled.

- Technical and market research depends on information. Remote viewing boosts this capability. Benchmarking, copying the best features of your competitor's products and services and incorporating them into your own company's products and services, requires a good supply of information about those competitors. Remote viewing and sensing is the best way of spying on competitors. Even better is to use future RV to appropriate next-generation technology and products from decades ahead.

- To develop ideas based on remote viewing information, 'garage research' is needed to develop microclimates of opportunity for the marketplace. This is reverse engineering future technology, so it works with primitive present day components.

- Production and product development depends on information. New developments in production technology that radically changed performance and competitiveness used to come once every 20 years, and now they come once every three years. Soon they will come once a year. A company and organisation needs a good supply of uncorrupted information to survive these times of rapid change. Remote viewing and sensing enables a company to steal inventions from the future. By this means psiops companies will dominate the world markets, as those who do not take up psiops will be put out of business.

- Total quality management (TQM) depends on precise guidelines and a commitment to excellence. The aim of TQM is the delivery of products and services with zero defects. Psiops information systems using remote viewing on near future production technology in their field should provide staff with the information on precisely what is called for, rather than ill-defined desires. TQM is a very precise science and depends on a large body of knowledge to get things right. Future RV of how to do this will prove invaluable.

- Products and services should be available on demand. Customers should be able to get what they want as quickly as possible. To do this the organisation must have real-time information on clients' needs. teamworking based on management nodes should get products and services into the marketplace with the minimum of bottlenecks. Use remote viewing and sensing to find these mystery problems.

- Make it easy for the customer to do business. Allow the customer control over the product and service so it fits their need and cost criteria. Use psiops information systems to help your customer do this by making it easy for the customer to contact you. Allowing the producer to communicate with the customer via your psiops information system also increases your organisation's sales power and enables customers and you to cut out middlemen. Ensure that information about defects in your products is promptly sent to the relevant personnel in real-time. This enables faults and other things of importance to be handled in real-time. RS facilitates all the above.

- Sales and marketing departments depend on information for orders, brochures and advertising – amongst other things. Psiops information systems increase their ability to react at speed. In a crowded marketplace it is vital to make your product or service special. Being second or third behind a competitor can cost the company a fortune, because everyone remembers the first in a field of endeavour, and the also-rans are forgotten. Psiops management information systems allow the organisation to beat its competitor to the punch by using remote viewing of future technology to jump decades ahead. First to market means profitability in many cases, since psiops companies and organisations are also cautious; they do not follow fashion with 'me too' products, which turn out to be white elephant endeavours. Psiops organisations make money by being the first and best. Making the organisation prosper in real-time is the goal!

Cells in the supercell and autonomous action

As discussed previously, allowing staff to use their initiative is necessary if the organisation is to work in real-time. Referring all decisions to higher levels of management leads to organisational gridlock. But giving staff their autonomy can be traumatic at first. There are three main negative memes. These problems are:

- Staff have been conditioned from school days to follow orders from their superiors. In many cases initiative has been stifled by supervisors who do not like 'their people' getting above themselves.

- In many cases staff do not know what to do because the job has been so poorly defined.

- Some staff like to be given orders so they cannot be blamed for any mistakes they have made based on their own initiative.

Faced with problems such as these, psiops managers need to appreciate that historical factors are against them. In the past, staff were given routinely repetitive tasks that fitted in with the production line mentality of the time. Schools churned out obedient wage slaves and workers knew their place. Psiops requires staff to work in an almost diametrically opposed way. Reengineering the organisation to eliminate old obsolete working practice must, if it is to be effective, address the old stereotype that staff have been following and replace it with one geared to psiops. Meme theory is vital in this context.

A prerequisite is for all staff to think of their jobs as a

vocations rather than drudgery. Only when staff have this point of view will their true potential be harnessed to the organisation in a way that is beneficial for both. To do this, we must first look at how people get on together. We are communal creatures. Ancient people went round in groups. Survival prospects for the individual were increased when he or she was part of a clan or tribe.

Autonomous action memes

The first principle of autonomy is to **have effective team-working throughout the organisation**. Relationships must be based on mutual respect and trust in the abilities of others.

The second principle of autonomy is to **arrange these teams into groups of a workable size**, with between three and six members. This promotes mutual dialogue and group identity among team members. (Such groups are called staff cells.)

The third principle of autonomy is to **link each cell with another one**, and to get them to talk to each other regularly.

The fourth principle of autonomy is **never to give one group the opportunity to dominate another**.

The fifth principle of autonomy is to **have, in each staff cell, at least one member who likes to work on their own**. Some people like to be directed and will constantly ask what to do and how to do it. Others dislike being told what to do. Having a mix of these two types means that the cell is able to act on its own initiative. People who like to help others and give advice are necessary ingredients in a successful cell. A wise manager realises that people have a mix of characteristics within them. Careful nurturing can make dependant staff self-supporting, isolated staff into good team-workers and bossy staff diplomatic and willing to hear other points of view. Again, making staff cells work together in pairs helps, because each member of staff is seen not only by their own little group but by other groups. Peer pressure will eliminate bad traits within the working environment. The problem of persistently disruptive, lazy or incompetent staff must, however, be faced; there may be no place for them.

The sixth principle of autonomy is **subsidiarity: making decisions at the lowest possible level**. Passing decision-making up the management ladder obstructs effective action. An organisation based on the principle of subsidiarity can react quickly.

The seventh principle of autonomy is to **make staff cells responsible for their own quality control**; this is the established practice of total quality management. As mentioned earlier, peer group pressure aids in getting all team members working together to the required standard. Of course, this puts an obligation on managers to lay down clearly defined standards. Laxity on the part of managers will have a bad effect on workers, as they will not be sure how they stand with respect to the job and a state of affairs where staff are unsure will lead to anxiety, setting in train a destructive feedback cycle.

The eighth principle of autonomy is **job flexibility**. Rotation of jobs stimulates interest as staff do not keep doing the same thing every day. Interest in the job is a prime requisite for turning a job into a vocation, which in itself is a prerequisite for optimal performance. An additional benefit is that work is not disrupted if one individual happens to be away.

The ninth rule of autonomy is to **promote a culture of continuous improvement**. People constantly come up with good ideas and ways of doing their job better in a psiops organisation; staff have a milieu in which their individuality can be harnessed to improve performance and conditions in the workplace.

The tenth rule of autonomy concerns feedback to managers from staff cells. **Continual interference by management will hinder, not help performance**. Psiops managers, as they can remotely sense, trust the staff cells which they serve, delegate as far as possible and empower them to do their jobs as well as they can.

Supercells

From what has been said previously, it is easy to see that people working with 'strangers' in large groups feel isolated and alone. This tends to reinforce any personal destructive cycles; hence the illness, absenteeism and poor performance in the larger groups. As discussed previously, a psiops organisation should aim to group staff into 'supercells' composed of around 80 to 150 people who can know each other personally, with periodic rotation of individual staff and staff cells within the supercell. Rotation of managers is also beneficial, since it keeps horizontal management lines extending throughout the organisation, and, for the same reason, regular meetings between managers of different supercells are also desirable.

Production lines and conventional offices have traditionally worked by splitting tasks into simple, repetitive routines which unskilled staff could perform with a minimum of training. From the point of view of the managers, this way of working had the advantage that monitoring and supervision are simple. Unfortunately for the advocates of this method of working, people were not robots that would happily perform mindless, repetitive tasks year after year. In fact, it promoted negative attitudes and alienation; strikes, illness and absenteeism. How people are required to act throughout the day has a profound effect on company culture: boring, mindless work makes staff pernickety and stressed.

To establish psiops in an organisation, the nature of work has to be changed. Fortunately, it is now widely recognised that the division of labour into its smallest possible parts is an obsolete concept. Lean production is an accepted method of improving performance; workers share the task of building an entire item, such as a car. As well as making workers feel more involved and committed to their work, making one member of staff responsible for a whole job instead of part of a job can be much more efficient – the time spent communicating with other members of staff is eliminated. Errors caused as orders are passed down the chain are also reduced; having staff learn many memes rather than repeat one meme continuously is more natural to them and therefore more efficient.

This state of affairs promotes a positive meme cycle. Company culture is transformed into the positive, benevolent state filled with the positive memes required for psiops management. Memes of success and feelings of belonging and well-being are spread through company gossip, while negative memes of absenteeism, illness and accidents are reduced in the organisation.

But this type of working requires flexible, intelligent staff, and to manage them successfully, old methods based on the production line mentality must be abandoned.

This optimised way of doing the job is the 'virus of good practice' in psiops meme. It is characterised by:

- Looking at the entire task, be it making a car or fulfilling an order. Use RV and RS to optimise it. Use future RV/RS to better the best in the present.

- Realising optimal efficiency is only achieved if staff have positive attitudes inculcated by RS of what gets staff motivated.

- Systematising the job to the point where staff know exactly what they have to do and are trained for all possible contingencies. This turns our activity into a mode of operation where staff feel confident they can do the task and are 'up to speed' in all its details. Use future RV to optimise this.

- Making staff so confident of their own personal working practices that they are able to teach others exactly how to duplicate it. Use RS for this. The good working practice has now become self replicating – just like a virus.

As mentioned previously, the main proponents of this style of management are military organisations. They apply the 'four man rule'; two groups of four are used by the SAS and SBS as the basic combat unit, deployed behind enemy lines to spread 'alarm and despondency', a euphemism for mayhem and murder. Army companies consist in general of three combat-ready platoons each of 30 to 40 men under the commander and his staff – a total of around 150 men, that magic number again. The military company is a good example of a supercell.

These well understood working practices will hopefully be copied by example throughout the organisation, for 'imitation is the highest form of flattery'; people who perform their work competently will be copied by their well-motivated colleagues. Military organisations have much to teach civilians in this matter. They train their personnel to the highest standard. Every mission is rehearsed beforehand until it has been perfected. Combat troops train in the environment they will actually be fighting in. Beach landings in occupied territory, for example, are not only practised by the sea, but also in the same terrain at the same time of night and at the correct phase of the moon as it will be at the planned date of the attack. Live ammunition is normally used to simulate being under fire and hence stimulate stress, so those involved can come to terms with it before the action. Contingency plans are devised for worst case scenarios and the personnel are trained for them. After the mission, a thorough debriefing takes place to discover how it was completed and what lessons could be learned; these are quickly assimilated and applied.

The military model described above has obvious benefits for real-time organisations. Let us now see how we can usefully apply this to our civilian organisation.

1. Our command staff are now the management nodes in psiops. These nodes register:
   a) An overview of what going on in their departments based on their personal experience.
   b) Information, via remote sensing, of what is going on in the organisation as a whole, together with new information that has a bearing on their jobs and those of their staff, gained by remote viewing of future new technology.
   c) Unforeseen circumstances, caused primarily by the chaotic environment, which are avoided by remote viewing and sensing.

2. Information and memes passing through the management node is analysed by RS. This can be classified into six categories:
   a) Information and memes concerning ways of acting, presenting ideas and imagery, which actively promote feelings of success and positive attitudes – optimised by RS.
   b) Information and memes on management techniques acquired by personal experience and education can be improved by future RV.
   c) Organisational knowledge and memes gained by being part of the organisation and training.
   d) Personal development memes: this includes empathy, knowledge of how people tick, relationships within the organisation, RS, as well as conventional personnel management.
   e) Training memes, which are the sum total of all jobs previously done – optimised by RS and future RV.
   f) Cultural memes, gained from your upbringing and

country as well as all the company cultures experienced, uprated by RS of the future. All these aspects of management have to be fine-tuned in order to lead staff. RS is the key to success – future RV the ace in the hole.

3. All managers have a great deal of knowledge and power that can be used to enable staff to do their jobs. Yet all this is worth nothing if the manager cannot put himself in the staff's shoes. Remote sensing enables the psiops manager to empathise and mind read. Many fine management initiative memes have floundered on this rock of misperception. Information and courses of action have to be changed when they leave the management node and pass to those in the front line.

4. Total quality management memes should become habitual. To this end the psiops management organisation transmits memes that facilitate:
   a) Pre-shift briefings.
   b) Team working.
   c) Continuous improvement seminars.
   d) Performance workshops where staff can spread their knowledge and expertise to reinforce successful methods of working. General rules for cultivating the meme or the virus of good practice in an organisation for managers and staff are as follows:
      i) Define your objective in a detailed, systematic manner.
      ii) Run through all the contingencies that come about from the best, mean and worst case scenarios.

iii) Train staff and managers under the actual conditions they will experience.

iv) Optimise the plan to achieve the objective in the most effective way.

5. Practise this optimal plan until it is second nature to all staff.

6. Give full support to staff and managers whilst they are carrying out the objective.

7. Thoroughly debrief staff and managers after completion of the project.

8. Ensure staff and managers pass on their experience to inexperienced staff, and involve these experienced staff in training. Monitor the whole process by RS to see what steps grate on staff. Optimise the procedure until the staff have no problems with the protocols.

The above meme principles apply to industrial production. Since production engineering is changing at an ever-quickening pace, new skills are always needed in the factory. Staff cells in psiops also require a broad knowledge of skills to work effectively. To this end the principles can be adapted from their general form to fit psiops production management memes. Use future RV to improve on all aspects of the process listed below:

1. Define how the product will be built.

2. Refine the production process for quality and efficiency.

3. Make sure this is carried out on the factory floor, not under conditions so controlled that they could never be achieved.

4. Allow the staff cells to refine their own working practices.

5. Do not be satisfied until the product is no less than perfect for the market.

6. Give the staff cells and managers everything they need for the job.

7. Debrief staff and managers so lessons learnt can quickly be disseminated throughout the organisation using RS.

For an organisation to prosper, it is essential that it should have clearly defined objectives, with everyone aligned to these goals – RS enables this process to run smoothly.

Organisational evolution, economic benchmarking and the rate-determining step

To restructure an organisation for psiops management, we look for simple principles that can aid the manager. An organism does not suddenly adapt itself due to rapidly changing environmental events: organisms evolve. Similarly, organisations have to evolve; they resist discontinuous change.

Restructuring thus involves organisational evolution (OE).

Organisational evolution meme

1. Learn to see the world as it is, which is aided by remote viewing and sensing. Learn how to see the future by use of RV/RS.

2. Transform the negative feedback cycle to a positive cycle, using the 12 meme principles of psiops management, motivation and success, all discussed previously.

3. Cut down reliance on conventional long-term strategic planning and instead use Adaptive Strategic Planning and remote viewing. Realising that the world is changing too rapidly for accurate prediction except by remote viewing, top executives attempt to optimise the probability of long-term projects succeeding no matter what happens. This needs effective remote viewers, but the advantage is that costly mistakes are avoided. Future RV enables them to leap ahead of the competition.

4. Clearly define aims by pursuing MCOs with alacrity, acquisitiveness and total commitment using remote viewing of future technology. The more MCOs an organisation has, the better its future prospects and present-day performance. But an organisation that pursues MCOs has to evolve in order to fulfil them using remote viewing and, more importantly, RS to steer the optimal path.

5. Finding MCOs needs an excellent ability to remote view the future. This depends on the individuals within the organisation being psiops managers. Managers of all varieties within the organisation have good ideas. In

non-psiops organisations the corporate body is slow to appreciate them. A psiops organisation welcomes iconoclasm when it comes to dogma and obsolete ways of thinking and seeing the world. On the other hand, the psiops organisation teaches managers the need to get on with other members of the organisation, to stimulate positive memes and attitudes as well as group RV and RS on subjects of interest from the present and future. Iconoclastic but not anti-social, is the attribute needed for seekers of MCOs in a psiops organisation.

6. Lean management allows horizontal and vertical feedback, which enables psiops management. Managers who apply it also have the time to think about MCOs and look for them with future remote viewing. Filling managers' days up with mindless supervisory tasks instead of trusting staff groups to control their own work is a sure recipe for stagnation.

7. Once potential MCOs are identified, there must be scope within the organisation to develop inner virtual reality by remote viewing, then to see whether they are viable in the marketplace. If possible, deploy small research teams on site to carry out 'garage research', working in conjunction with the RV 'inventor' of the idea. In an organisation that has financial difficulties, roving research teams can perform a similar function, re-engineering future technology for client companies.

8. Restructuring in its formal sense has two aspects: the redesign of sub-processes and making people's jobs as interesting as possible. Intelligent, adaptable staff are

required for this new way of working – enabled by effective application of RS.

9. Staff cells are a core competency of the psiops organisation. An organisation that has highly intelligent, flexible personnel that can RV and RS can carry out many different types of business.

10. Organisational evolution: one reason company culture has so much inertia is the education system that most people have been through. Autonomous action has been suppressed by the teaching establishment, whilst obedience to orders has been rewarded. This mentality was useful for the production line but is inimical to psiops. Simply telling people to get on with the job with little or no supervision does not work as staff flounder with things they do not really understand. Psiops management transforms this negative meme structure to a positive meme one. Organisational evolution therefore requires very specific ways of dealing with staff, based on meme theory. In line with their education, re-engineer the organisation by using memes to:
    a) Ensure that staff realise that the psiops management nodes are now giving the orders – augmented by RV/RS.
    b) Recognise that 'fuzzy logic' applies in using RV/RS. There is not necessarily a right or wrong decision, so aim to make the best decision at every step of the way, or if there is insufficient information available, make the most reasonable decision based on RV/RS.
    c) Encourage feedback to psiops management nodes,

to allow staff to optimise their RV/RS performance. Use those psiops management nodes as information and service centres for RV/RS, enabling them to do their job better.

d) Once the normal mode of operation has been optimised by RV/RS, staff are allowed to get on with their job without further interference from management. They understand what they are doing and how to do it.

e) Recognise that people have been designed to be adaptable and will live up to any ideal as long as the innovator realises they are human. Their bounded rationality needs to be developed to suit their needs, and in doing so will fall into line with the innovator's scheme of things. All innovators should realise this or they will fail. People are people and you cannot change them, but they can allow themselves to change and will do so if given a clearly defined goal and the incentive to reach it. All organisational evolution depends on this driving force, knowledge of meme theory and RS.

11. Psiops restructuring requires that the organisation has clearly defined goals at every level. Optimise goals by RV. This calls for clear definition of the memes of the modes of operation needed to achieve it. Optimise memes by RS.

12. Economic benchmarking: in many organisations the goals of the organisation are limited by the customers' desire for low-cost products. Many grand schemes and ideas fail here. Economic benchmarking production

(EBP) is therefore necessary to make sure that organisational evolution is aligned with the marketplace and customers' needs; the best ideas come to nothing if no one can afford them. Quality in this context is about giving customers what they want and no more, as quality can cost money. Use of future RV to get technology to cut costs is essential.

Below is a general overview of psiops economic benchmarking. Though it does not directly speed up the working of the organisation, it does indirectly for the organisation has to work in real-time and have future RV technology acquisition for economic benchmarking to be effective. The main points of economic benchmarking apply to a psiops organisation as follows:

a) Psiops information networks are used to discover what the customer is prepared to pay. Once this is known, the organisation can set price targets.

b) The task of EBP product development is assigned to selected management nodes with the appropriate skills of RV/RS. These management nodes evaluate alternative EBP schemes and select and refine the most promising using RV/RS.

c) Garage research, with future remote viewing to help erase snags, is used to develop good ideas originating from the psiops management nodes and those staff cells with experience in this line of work. In this way, projects can be brought to the stage where they are ready for a pilot run.

d) In the light of this pilot scheme, the scale of production can be stepped up to the level required.

e) Feedback from the customer is needed at all stages

of the development process, so that EBP can be for the market.

The rate-determining step in psiops

To conclude this introduction to restructuring for psiops, let us consider how, in the light of all that has been discussed, an organisation can speed up its reaction time. The goal of any organisation should be to achieve real-time operation.

'Time benchmarking' is a good starting point: matching reaction time to the strongest competitors in your market sector. But since few organisations have achieved real-time operation, time benchmarking will not result in a real-time management organisation; all it will do is make the organisation as fast or a little faster than its competitors. Only by remotely viewing future competitors can the quantum leap be made to real-time business, something the US military is developing for the battlefield, used in the most recent war in Iraq.

What is needed is a systematised method of reducing the reaction time in any organisation, to such an extent that real-time management is possible. A good analogy is a chemical reaction, where processes may consist of a sequence of steps. The slowest step controls the maximum speed at which the overall process will run. This is called the rate-determining step. Increasing the speed of other steps in the sequence is useless. The same principle applies in organisations and business. In any sequential, multi-stage operation, the rate-determining step controls its overall speed.

To find the rate-determining step in any process necessitates:

1. The managers and members of the psiops management nodes fully understanding the process and the feeder processes leading up to it. Use RV and RS to get an overview. Use future RV to look for something that better fits the bill.

2. That they ask the staff about the day-to-day practicalities of the process.

Once this is done the rate-determining step can be identified, speeded up or bypassed altogether. Once the bottleneck has been located, eliminated or optimised so that it is no longer the rate-determining step, management nodes can move their attention to the next slowest step, since this has become rate-determining. The above tactic of elimination or optimisation is repeated, over and over again, until the overall process has been optimised. This is the time-benchmarked goal. This meme is replicated throughout the company.

Top executives can oversee the implementation of these tactics throughout the organisation, aided by remote viewing and sensing. Once this has been achieved, further work is needed to dovetail all the processes together into a coherent whole. To this end, the rate-determining steps in the organisation as a whole should be ruthlessly eliminated or optimised as applicable, by use of RV and RS.

Review of psiops management

Psiops management, as we have seen, has two main aspects. The first deals with RV and RS. Secondly, it reappraises management theory in the light of advances in our understanding of how people interact. This uses, to some extent, scientific techniques derived from military advances in remote viewing, such as future RV for appropriating future technology. The CIA told me they called this technical remote viewing and have released only 1 per cent of their findings to the public. All the RV protocols they had released previously could be blocked out. I hope this book enables non-military users to access the same resource, except this is a next-generation version unblockable even by the military.

We conclude with a checklist which gives a brief summary of some of the signposts that a manager should keep in mind. The concept of a pre-flight mental reminder provides the framework around which the manager can build up a picture of psiops management – the flight being that of a remote viewer/sensor to wherever and whenever she or he wishes to go. Readers who have got this far have proved themselves keen and intelligent and may have seen ways of improving on the ideas that we have talked about. The following checklist for psiops management is given to enable the manager to begin to apply psiops management memes.

1. People do not work like robots, but are limited by bounded rationality. This can, however, be optimised for the work at hand. To use RS to empathise and see into their mindset is invaluable.

2. Feedback from staff is essential. The more feedback in an organisation, the easier and more accurately its workings can be monitored, and the quicker it can react to widely changing circumstances. RS enables true feedback on what is really going on.

3. Microclimates of opportunity exist even in the worst of times. To thrive in difficult times the company must hunt out microclimates of opportunity energetically and establish the infrastructure to take advantage of them before its competitors. Remote viewing of the future is useful in this context.

4. 'Quick and dirty' research of future technology gained by RV by good research and development staff is a prerequisite for developing microclimates of opportunity for the marketplace.

5. Organisational evolution (OE) enables an organisation to adapt to changes in its environment. A fluid approach to strategic planning, using RV coupled with OE, makes possible the constant evaluation of ongoing and long-term projects. Remote viewing the future enables the psiops manager to steer a safe path through the minefield of real business life.

6. Once psiops management memes have been introduced into an organisation it is useful to be able to monitor how the reaction time of the organisation is improving. Each manager can make up a list of key indicators that apply to their organisation and see how they improve. RS is the key to this.

7. Psiops management can enhance the core business in many ways, allowing customers' needs to be recorded and responded to in the most effective way, by use of RV and RS.

8. Adaptability: adaptable infrastructures, modes of operation and staff are prerequisites for survival. Adapting to use RV and RS in business is a case in point.

9. Since organisations exist to satisfy their customers' needs, they should steer clear of negative feedback cycles, office politics and tunnel vision, which can turn a profitable company with good products into a 'basket case'. RS achieves this.

10. All around us organisations are floundering as they struggle to keep pace with changes in the world. An organisation able to remotely view the future and use RS to react in real-time can become an island of stability, and attract customers who crave a sense of order.

11. Psiops management is so important to the long-term future of an organisation that it should become the archetype to which infrastructure is shaped. Building in all we have talked about in this book to good companies will take time but will be acceptable to those highly motivated managers who realise market instability and long-term unpredictability requires psiops management, and the ability to remotely view and sense in a world at war.

12. Total quality management (TQM) – the technology and skills to make fault-free products for the customers – has been the bane of all slipshod staff and managers. Applying the principles of future RV to TQM and to tactical planning within departments and organisations gives a good indication of where bad decision making is

occurring. In combination with RS, this allows the manager to apply proven techniques and practices to projects, so they can see their good ideas being utilised immediately. This injects success into projects, breeding a culture of success which feeds on itself and becomes self-sustaining.

13. Psiops information networks: use of RV and RS are needed to gather all the relevant data on customers so their needs can be fulfilled in the shortest possible time. Similarly psiops real-time management information networks using RV and RS allow management to build up an accurate picture of their organisation so staff can be serviced with resources and backup as well as possible.

14. Company culture limits the performance of organisations. The principles of psiops management (applications of RS), success memes and motivation memes are the first steps towards optimising company culture.

15. Supercells, composed of around 150 people, are the ideal size for social cohesion. Likewise, groups of four are ideal for conversation and therefore serve as the basic unit of the management node which can be used for group RV/RS. Incorporating the natural units of group interaction into company structure leads to an organisation that feels 'right' and can best use the talents of its personnel in RV/RS. This configuration provides the perfect matrix for feedback both in a vertical and horizontal plane.

16. An organisation that does not understand how its personnel function and does not understand meme theory will not only be slow in reacting, it will also be inefficient in satisfying its customers' needs. It will be blind to opportunities and MCOs that present themselves and will forever follow behind its competitors.

17. Psiops organisations understand the human dynamic, meme structures and their ·importance for success. Catering to the needs of personnel is the core competency of a psiops company as this promotes a positive meme cycle. Similarly, the psiops organisation understands its customers and through advertising, promotion and development tailors its image and product to promote positive memes and attitudes – to do this one needs RS.

The above principles of psiops memes can be put in a personal context for the manager, as follows:

1. Take account of people's aspirations and optimise to everyone's benefit using RS.

2. Listen to all staff – use RS.

3. Look for opportunities in all areas using RV.

4. Use simple tests to sift the dross from the nuggets of great ideas by use of RV to see if they work. Use future RV to get new ideas.

5. Keep an eye on your department by RS and see how it

fits in with what is going on around it by RV.

6. In your department, make things improve all the time by using RV and RS.

7. Remember that speed is of the essence. Look into the future using RV.

8. Be adaptable, develop psiops and use RS in all human interactions.

9. Be first on the draw to satisfy your customer by using future RV of technology. Use RS to implement the whole process successfully.

10. Cultivate the skill to be fast and first, by use of psiops – future RV/RS.

11. Remember that psiops managers think of themselves as centres of psiops management, facilitating this goal wherever they go. They have a clear view of everything that pertains to their business as they are adept at RV/RS.

12. Constantly strive to improve the quality of your decisions by self RS and RV of their outcomes.

13. Understand the organisation and your customers by using RS.

14. Know how to satisfy your customers by using RV to look into the future to map demand.

15. Ensure that you are pigeonholed as a successful individual – a psiops manager – by RS your effect on other people.

16. Learn remote viewing and sensing, then apply them to your business whilst accessing the future to reverse engineer their technology, ideas and science – RV science.

TEN

PSIOPS AND THE INVESTOR

Russell Targ, one of the CIA's top remote viewers, (when he left Stanford Research Institute) used RV to increase the yields of people investing in the stock market. We will now look at how to remotely view the future to increase your probability of buying and selling the right shares, bonds, commodities and futures. Following on from this is a discussion of how RS and RI can be used by the psiops adept for investment analysis and to influence markets, personnel and sales figures in the business world. The use of RS and RI to affect the money markets may have implications for the investor. Psiops, such as remote viewing and how to use RI to raise or lower share prices, may be one of the most powerful uses of this advanced psiops technology.

Anticipating market trends is in essence the fundamental principal of good trading. There is, in a sense, nothing paranormal about anticipating future events. The basis of anticipating future events is based upon many things: projecting future trends and spotting new trends when they occur – before your competitors do. Disperse new memes so one knows which companies will soon be hot properties (in the way that spotting which arcade video games would be in demand for the home would have shown the investor that Nintendo was a good company to buy into). These memes are ways of acting and thinking which behave rather like computer viruses – the fashion industry is based on them. For example, stacked shoes were fashionable when I was a teenager in the 1970s. They are fashionable again, thanks to media idols, especially female pop groups, which themselves represent a powerful meme that is rising in women – girl power.

The investor uses intuition as a valuable tool to map the future. Intuition though, is not as simple as it may seem. One can think of the paranormal as being a superset of intuition. The paranormal, as used by the psiops adept for precognitive remote viewing (PRV), is effectively an augmented and systematised approach to a scientific basis for intuition. Precognitive remote viewing develops intuition in an ordered way.

Nor is the simple extrapolating and mapping of future events in one's brain a process that cannot be markedly improved by the use of PRV. Manufacturers' product development can be helped by having managers who can mentally map the process to a better extent than their competitors. Sales forces should be able to radically improve their sales targets by using RS and RI. Using RS to discern why the market makes one sort of purchasing decision rather than another is another valid use. This leads us on to investments.

Securities and equities depend on the market. Trading in any area of endeavour may be greatly enhanced by PRV. For example, markets can be thought of as the summation of people's desires. To understand what drives these desires, we need to use RS to study the processes going on in the brains of selected samples of the demographic we wish to influence. Having the ability to remotely sense the group mind by using PRS can prove to be of great benefit to the investor.

In this respect, PRV may be of use to the investment sector. Stocks, bonds, futures, commodities, derivatives and other investment opportunities have long been thought of as a gamble. In reality, these investments depend on the mood of the market and confidence in the company, commodity or bond.

RV and RS may be of use in the financial sector, dependant as it is on perceived reality, rather than actual reality.

Unlike the lottery or betting on the horses, the wise and informed investor can make a consistent profit in the financial markets. PRV enables people who have an interest in markets to increase the percentage of correct investments they make. I am no expert in the details of the market, but the applied use of psi-technology may enable the reader to experiment with some RV techniques that could make an expert investor even richer. Since psiops is unknown in the marketplace, and the top-secret US parapsychological black projects seem to lack a real scientific knowledge about this new technology as applied to the investment field, the author hopes to enable the reader to become one of the market leaders in this field of endeavour. Influencing the market, and getting into the minds of market makers, may be possible.

It is well known that the mood of the market can be influenced by the big players. Large investors who have staff that can remotely view will enable these big players to have another avenue of information which their competitors lack. Inside knowledge of takeovers, government policy changes and multinationals' future plans can enable the investor to make large profits in a relatively short space of time. A knock-on effect of remote viewing is that it enables the psi-operator to get into the mindset of the individual, government or company he wishes to second-guess. The practise of psiops also enables the investor to increase the speed and number of mental simulations that can be run in the brain. One of the effects of this may be to increase the RV investor's intelligence, intuition and precognition.

Further to this, the use of RS can enable the investor to 'get into the head' of the CEO, minister or board of directors he wishes to understand. This enables the RS investor to begin to get ideas and feelings about what the people he is interested in are about to do. It also gives the RS investor the ability to see the mindset of all the major players in his sector of the market.

Psiops does not guarantee that PRV and RS will give a 100 per cent accurate picture of all the future and secret plans of organisations of interest, but experience shows that the investor will get a marked increase in successful hunches about what the competitor or a major player will do.

Looking at the stock market, the value of shares which are of interest to the investor may either go up or down in price. Using RV, one may be able to get valuable clues as to what will happen to the share price of the stock one finds of interest. RS of the major players in this stock can also allow the wise investor the ability to know what will happen to that specific share price in the near future. This allows the RV investor to sell or buy, depending on the situation. Enhanced mentation available to the psiops investor could enable the RV practitioner to make the best of this new information channel.

Commodities are dependant on many factors which governments are usually privy to. Remote viewing of government reports before they are officially published may enable the RV investor to be several steps ahead of the market.

Psiops, as applied to group minds, may also be of interest, although the group mind of the market depends on the cultural and neurolinguistic software, hardwired into the brain. This, in turn, is dependant on the neurones competitively branching out and competing with each other in brain development; the selective death of neurones and mental pathways that are not used. In effect, every one of our cultures carries a neural network defined by the memes it consists of: cultural memes that spread through populations; and new memes that change the marketplace. These are driven by the nexus point humanity is approaching, as a whole gamut of problems converge on the early 21st century.

Remote influencing of the group mind may be possible. One caveat would be the problem that any person who is part of the group mind may find it impossible to psychically influence the group mind to any meaningful extent. This is due to an isolated system not being able to know itself accurately, due to there being blind spots in the perception of the whole. Therefore RI, and for that matter RS, would require the psi-operator to step outside of the group consciousness. This may prove impossible for the investor, who needs to keep track of the market and go with the flow. To this end, hiring the psiops adept who are not enmeshed in the rat-race of the market, might prove highly beneficial. To remotely influence group minds one requires large amounts of energy and a high level of expertise. Once any meaningful remote influence can be generated to significantly affect markets, the investor has an immensely powerful tool at his disposal. It ought, in principal, to have substantial effects on the markets in certain cases.

Derivatives, because they are secondary investments, depend on people forming judgements about what might happen (betting on the outcome of an event), and are much more vulnerable to RI. The more layers of perception and decision making between the group mind and actual reality, the more amenable that market is to psi-generated RI. Derivatives are getting so complicated that it may take the enhanced mental faculties of psi-practitioners to begin to understand this sector of the market. American and Russian theoretical physicists have been hired by US investment companies to get their minds around the problem of derivatives. Such is the complexity of the factors involved in derivative trading that theoretical physicists, with their grasp of complex mathematical equations, are best suited to deal in them.

Similarly, the bond market may be more profitable to the investor if that person has access to psiops. Since interest rates set by the Federal Reserve and the Bank of England influence the world's economy and markets, remotely viewing these meetings allows the psiops-adept to trade effectively.

An overview of psiops for the investor

Projection of awareness outside one's body has up until now been a subjective phenomena. With an understanding of the nature of RV, a scientific rationale which explains this phenomena has become available.

As we have seen, a relaxed state of mind is the first step in setting up RV. Knowledge of the mechanisms involved in lowering the frequency of brain rhythms is the vital second step. After which DA ensues. This DA can be used to focus on the investment opportunity, to get a sense of the underlying factors that control the price of that share, stock or bond. Awareness can then be projected out of the body to examine the future price of that investment, this being the basis of precognitive remote vision.

Checklisting the sensory input one gets from PRV of that investment as it develops in time can give useful information on what the future price of that investment opportunity may be. Directed attention fixated on investments you know well gives rise to remote viewing. Repeated use of this awareness develops the precognitive remote viewing phenomena. Sending your awareness to remotely view investments of special interest is the next step. The more this technique is practised, the stronger one's remote viewing attention becomes.

Directed attention can then grow to the point where one can remotely view documents of interest and even access computer data by remote viewing. By this method one can get inside information on the future of a company, such as mergers, before it is made public.

Crop yields which affect futures markets can also be remotely viewed, and this may enable the astute investor to make a great deal on that particular futures investment.

Once the faculty of RV has come into being, awareness can be projected into other people. Analogous to the method Dr Simonton developed to enable cancer patients to become aware of their own immune system, remote viewers can learn to scan other people's brains using this application of remote viewing. Development of this faculty leads to remote sensing. By scanning the CEO and board of a particular company of interest, the investor should be able to predict the profitability or coming merger of that company with another, before it becomes public knowledge. By this means, decisions can be made upon whether to buy or sell shares in that particular company.

RS starts with the realisation that brain centres in the limbic system filter out the majority of sensory data we receive. Using DA, we can reprogram our brain centres – such as the thalamus – to let in all the information we receive. Then we have to reconfigure our mental models to fit this raw data into recognisable configurations we can perceive. The result is the development of awareness that can pick up usable data from other people's body language; sensing subliminal cues from all our senses that enable us to know things intuitively. The long-term effects of this defiltering process in the brain leads to visual perception of low-level photon emissions from the body; or, in simple terms, one sees auras.

Remote sensing can be used as a stepping stone to development of scanning abilities, either directly, or as precognitive scanning to see the future mindset of the people of interest. Conversely, remote sensing can be used to scan brain activity which is indicative of volitional action – by use of the SMA. This can enable the psi–adept to predict the decision making of CEOs and the boards of the companies of interest, in order to enable profitable investing. Remote sensing, coupled with memory scanning, can be used to identify people who are leaking information in an organisation. This enables the investor to predict how many other people in the market will know this information.

Remote influencing and investing

Remote sensing leads on to remote influencing. The most commonly used form of this is to plant suggestions in the market makers to 'talk up' the market, or 'talk down' the particular investment which is of interest to the psi-investor. They will use altered perception to predict what the market makers will do, then try to correct that decision so that it complies with the psiops investor's intent. RS of people leads on to the ability to identify mental blocks that enable that person to resist your telepathic hypnotic suggestions, after which they can be removed. The person you are scanning can then be remotely influenced. Directed attention on that mental block in the market maker allows the possibility of correcting that negative resistance to the psiops investor's remotely influenced suggestions. Knowledge of basic human physiology aids accurate remote sensing and develops remote influencing. With practise, one can learn to become very capable at using RS and RI to increase the likelihood of profitable investments. The knock-on effect of this is that the psi-abilities latent in the investor come more to the fore. With sustained practise, the psiops investor can influence the investments of interest to a greater and greater degree.

Remote influencing enables us to have very powerful market making abilities, which can be used to help our portfolio of investments. So not only PRV, but the growing ability of the psi-investors to utilise RI of brain centres, enables the practitioners to develop remote suggestion. This ability is the scientific basis of hypnosis. As with more primitive versions of hypnosis, not all people are susceptible – which is probably a good thing! Even so, use of this technique can considerably enhance investment opportunities;

sales techniques can also be enhanced by RI and could therefore be of use to anyone who has to sell goods or ideas to critical customers. Understanding the mechanism behind hypnosis allows people who have learnt RI to enhance the capabilities of other people. An example of this is the use of telepathic hypnotists in investment to enhance the performance of one's investment team.

Psi is dependent on projection of biophysical awareness, and since mechanistic scientists have decreed that the 'mind' does not exist, but is only a function of brain chemistry, they have concluded that psi cannot exist. Contrary to this view, the military have been working on psi for decades, developing RI that directly influences the brain. Much of the medical research for these phenomena was started by the Russians. RI research into the effects of extremely low frequency waves transmitted by biophysical fields as carrier beams showed that brains could be affected at a distance by 'telepathic radiation'. This telepathic suggestion mimics neurological processes in the brain which are naturally controlled by the market maker's own field phenomena in our investment cases. These fields are in fact biophysical phenomena. This means that the psi-investor, by becoming knowledgeable about morphogenetic fields, can increase the probability of people – and hence events – following his or her will. Psi can therefore aid the investor to increase the value of his or her portfolio, no matter what the market conditions. In a bear market, this can be of considerable use. The author has developed a working knowledge of these natural processes. This knowledge acts as the basis for this book and enables people to learn the basis of remote viewing, sensing and influencing, so that they have the groundwork to practise these techniques at their leisure.

The aim is to become a better investor by use of psi.

History of using psi for investment

In 1983 Russell Targ (formerly of Stanford Research Institute) and Keith Harary used RV to try and predict the prices of silver in the futures market. They wished to raise money for their psi-research. When they remotely viewed the silver futures, they had a resounding success, making money from their predictions. Their second attempt was not successful. They used a form of RV called associative remote viewing (ARV). In ARV, a remote viewer is told to look at the stock market advances or declines, or contracts won or lost, at some future date. The description given by the remote viewer is compared with future states predicted by computer models or experts in the market. The ARV outcome which most closely fits a certain particular future scenario of the market, is the one chosen. The simplest case is the scenario in which the remote viewer has to see whether the stock market will go up or down in the next month.

Dr Harold Puthoff, the head of CIA remote viewing research, used ARV to raise money for a children's school. This case of using ARV on the money markets was very successful. Rand De Mattei and Stephen Schwartz of the Mobius Society tried to use ARV to raise money for their research on psi-phenomena. They were not able to make a profit from their investments. It appears that when they became too personally concerned with the outcome, their ARV failed.

In the first ARV experiment, Targ and Harary were successful – they had carried out the ARV experiment with no preconceptions. Upon trying it again, their emotions were engaged and there was concern about the outcome. They failed. Emotional front-end-loading – being emotionally fearful that RV of the target must work – caused blockages which stopped successful RV. Emotional energy is part of the biophysical field. When you are concerned about the outcome, this emotional energy is used to create a meme which is programmed with the fear of failure. Since what you fear is attracted to you, this meme is designed to make your RV fail. Puthoff succeeded in using RV to make a profit because he was not emotionally linked with the children's school, so was not fearful of failure. Schwartz and De Mattei were emotionally involved with the success of their ARV, since they were trying to raise money for themselves.

Emotion plays a very large part in the RV process. Engineer Jack Houck, the American expert in psychokinesis, has carried out a number of experiments using ARV to predict the market. He does not tell his remote viewers about the market, he just asks them to remotely view a scene. He then compares that scene using a computer to make a decision about what will happen to the market in the time period concerned. Houck invests money by phoning his stockbroker, to get in and out of the market in a single day. Factors such as volatility, simplicity of transaction, volume, duration of investment, and insensitivity to a single investor, are considered. The Standard and Poore (S&P)100 Index and the (S&P) 500 Index, were chosen by Houck. He chose days when he thought the market would be volatile, but with little volume.

When Houck got his remote viewers together to look at the outcome of their group ARV, to see whether they had been successful, he told them to generate emotion and look at the picture of the correct market state for their ARV session – visualising their past selves remotely viewing that particular correct scene. Houck has discovered that the peak emotional event is transmitted through time and that RV seems to home in on this peak emotional event. The computer only transmits the correct target scene, so the group never see the wrong version that they might have remotely viewed. By this means, Houck hopes to cut down on transmission of incorrect images back through time, to the event when the remote viewers tried to foresee the future.

Houck's research has found that anyone who has seen wrong images of the target can send this information back through time, to interfere with the RV, directing the remote viewers' attention to the wrong version of reality. So strong is this effect, that the person using the computer to check on the RV sees only the correct picture of that target, so that they cannot inadvertently send this wrong version back through time to the remote viewers. A peak emotional event is designed to happen when the group see the target – if they have lost money this is rather hard to achieve. They place the picture of that particular market situation on permanent display, so that they can send the image back through time to their past selves who remotely viewed it.

This mixing of correct and failed targets means that emotional energy is sent back through time, no matter what the outcome. Houck has found that emotional energy has an attracting force on remote viewers' awareness. The author would postulate that the emotional charge sent back through time, no matter what the outcome, would confuse the biophysical field. This field is growing in awareness and is receiving an emotional charge whether it was right or wrong. By simple reward and punishment training, this technique is fatally flawed. An emotional charge should only be generated if a successful RV was achieved, to train the biophysical field to achieve primary consciousness – an awareness of its surroundings.

Practical precognitive remote viewing for the investor

When we begin to look at ways of using PRV for the money markets, it is important to first understand the rudiments of how they work. The bear market is one in which the values of the stocks and shares are dropping. Money can be made by selling before the market drops and buying back your original portfolio of stocks and shares for a fraction of their original price. If you tarry though, you will lose money. The Japanese and Far Eastern markets have collapsed. Hong Kong investors lost billions in a single day, the Japanese could potentially lose even more when their property collapse filters completely through the financial system. The crash of 2001 sparked by the 9/11 tragedy was an enormous loss of capital to all but the few investors of the elite who control the markets.

In a bull market the value of stocks and shares goes up. To make money in this type of market, you need to buy stocks and shares that will go up in price before the pack of traders discover them, raising the price by buying too many, which inflates the value of the stock or share. Early buyers make the money.

One can see that PRV is perfect for the money markets. Unlike US remote viewing technology, which is fixated on the right or wrong target, Russian psychotronics has a completely different philosophy. Russian psi-experts were not concerned with getting accurate, picture perfect, target images again and again and again. Psychotronics is mission-orientated: psi is used here to change reality, and is implemented repeatedly until an event comes about. An example might be remotely influencing a world leader so that he or she has a new set of ideas that affect his or her actions, so that Russia benefits. Unlike the right-or-wrong fixation of American RV, Russian psychotronics keeps on and on until the actual desired scenario comes about. Russians know psi exists, and so they do not have to endlessly prove it exists by trying to remotely view targets, then scoring themselves – the way so beloved of Western parapsychology.

In the Russian psychotronic method, the science behind psi is well known. What is important is using psiops to achieve the desired effect. Sustained use of psi is deployed until the desired result comes about. If the Russian psi adept wanted Saddam Hussein dead using remote killing, they would deploy more and more psi-assets to this mission, using psychotronic amplifiers to boost their RI until he was dead. US remote influencers tried to kill Saddam, but they failed, so they gave up – because it was 'obviously' not possible. In Russian psychotronics they would have redoubled their efforts and carried out research to see what psychic phenomena protected the tyrant. Since Russia is not an enemy of Iraq, this has never occurred.

In the case of the investor, the Russian model of psi – psychotronics – is the methodology needed for changing the markets to conform to your will. If US RV is used, the inevitable wrong remote viewing episodes will produce a lot of emotional energy which will produce negative memes, which interfere with correct PRV. Many of my students get very upset when they try RV and fail. This failure produces the negative memes which amplify the effect. That is why in my courses, I explain how RV works, so even though their RV might be hit and miss, they know it will improve if they duplicate the mechanisms which have been found to be behind the RV phenomena.

Using the Russian psychotronic model for investment, we take the completely opposite mental mindset to US experimenters. We study the market and get to understand the stocks and shares of interest. Magazines and books which teach us about the complexities of derivatives, buyouts, bonds, leverage and so on are read, to enable us to get a better mental model of the money markets. Once the investor feels comfortable with the market, he or she then uses PRV to study the stocks and shares of interest. Like a scientist who is experimenting in a new field, the investor begins to place small investments in the stocks and shares of interest. Success is something that is built up with time. The biophysical field must be raised from its latent state, to that of becoming aware of its surroundings – primary consciousness. Great interest in the market generates emotional energy, which trains the biophysical body to raise its consciousness so it can be aware of future share or stock prices. By this method a gradual evolution of the consciousness of the biophysical field takes place. The money market is a good way to train RV ability to develop in the biophysical field. Since it is a training programme, one does not expect immediate success. What is important is sustained interest in RV the market. This builds up the ability in the biophysical field to precognitively remotely view the money markets.

To use PRV for the money markets and to improve

business, the following protocols should be used:

Psiops protocols to begin precognitive remote viewing for the investor

1. A relaxed state of mind is the first step in setting up RV. To this end, baroque music should be played in the background to inculcate the alpha state of mind. A quiet room for RV should be set aside, where you have no distractions.

2. A vital second step is knowledge of the mechanisms involved in lowering the frequency of brain rhythms; the method by which the brain stress system can be altered by auto-visualisation.

3. Developing focused thought processes – directed attention – ensues. Enable the thalamus portion of the brain to generate the mental laser of DA which allows the brain stress system to be further modified. This will cause positive feedback, which allows the remote viewer to drop into theta at will. This mental state of theta is the doorway to psi, for it enables the remote viewer to shake off the negative effect of humanity's over-meme, the so-called PDF, which actively inhibits RV. One can use biofeedback devices which entrain this frequency of brain rhythm to reinforce this effect.

4. Directed attention can be used to focus on the biophysical field. The biophysical field can be boosted from its latent morphogenetic state to that of self awareness by using DA to empower the remote viewing energy fields. The intention of using the biophysical field for remote

viewing programmes the quantum computer within this body to carry out your brain's wishes.

5. Biophysical awareness can then be projected out of the body – the basis of remote viewing. Sending the bio-physical body to the future event to be studied in the money markets enables the biophysical field to pick up information from that future reality.

6. Checklisting the sensory input one gets from remote viewing in a systematic manner can give useful infor-mation upon which to begin modelling this future event in one's brain, so it can be predicted.

   We can change all aspects of our performance, thus being able to have 'the edge' over all our competitors. The first step is to list the perceptual cues we get when we try and remotely view a site of interest, eg:

tactile	* hard
	* glass screens
sounds	* noise of people talking and shouting
	* sound of footsteps
visual	* light
	* images of arithmetic figures
	* red or blue coloured lights next to them.

   In this way we can list the attributes of our remotely per-ceived site, so we can build a picture in our mind's eye of what it is. In the above case it was the London Stock Exchange.

7. Directed attention fixated on places you know, for

example the London Stock Exchange, gives rise to remote viewing perception of this specific area of awareness. Repeated use of this awareness develops the remote viewing phenomena, by instilling the biophysical field with the habit of psychically spying on the stock market; it continually travels to the Stock Exchange. This means that even while you are asleep, your biophysical field will travel to future Stock Exchange events, picking up PRV information upon which you can build up your picture of how the money markets will behave.

8. Sending your awareness to remotely view the future Stock Exchange whenever an event of interest occurs, is the next step. The more this technique is practised, the stronger one's remote viewing attention becomes. By homing in on the intense emotion generated by hectic days and key events in the money markets, you will be better able to predict when the market will have drastic falls or rises and therefore which are the most profitable times to sell or invest respectively.

Dealing with interference

Even when this RV process has been achieved, large amounts of interference will still be noticed by the remote viewing operator. Ingo Swann, the mentor of the US remote viewing 'Scan Gate' project, has come up with the signal-to-noise ratio idea. He has discovered that 80 per cent of the information gleaned by remote viewing was noise and only 20 per cent genuine information. I have discovered that by addressing the issue of stress and negative memes, the signal-to-noise ratio can be raised appreciably for the psi-investor.

I found that after people had been trained to operate in theta, it was necessary to optimise the memes people had acquired so that they could use remote viewing and its associated technologies. To recap, it was found that a considerable number of the memes we had acquired throughout our lives degraded remote viewing capacity and capability.

Knowledge of memes is of special interest in this area of investment. It is a well-known phenomena that there is a threshold of people or animals repeating the same meme, after which the meme becomes habitual to the race or species. The best example is the Japanese monkey that learns to wash the sand out of its wild rice by washing handfuls of it in the sea. Other members of its troop copy this meme.

Once a hundred or so of the monkey's peers have learnt to wash their rice, the meme miraculously appears in other monkey troops on other islands far removed from its original progenitor. The 'Hundredth Monkey' phenomena is a well-known anecdote about the spreading of memes by remote influencing. The market is dominated by these memes. If the remote viewer can tune into the prevailing memes influencing the market, then the future position of the market can be determined since ideas and what people believe are dominant factors in the money markets. Remote viewing the mindset of the market makers can give the remote viewer a good idea of what will occur in the future. RS and scanning of these market makers can build this rough mental sketch of the future state of the money market into a working model which enables sound investment.

Since many readers will not be rich investors, but instead will work for a living, the organisation they work within can benefit from this psiops investment technology.

This means that investment organisations that practise this remote viewing technology could find their entire company culture changing. Use of remote viewing in a company may increase mental efficiency, enhance immune responses, lessen anxiety and stress, and amplify the ability to intuit the correct path to success within the employees. Once the meme effect is put into practise, being able to remotely influence people around you in a positive manner – without you realising it – may result.

For remote viewing market activity, a listing of all negative and positive memes that affect the values of the stocks and shares being looked at is needed, so that they can be used to predict the future state of the market for investment purposes. Freeing up the biophysical energy needed for remote viewing within the psiops investor means that negative memes in the individual need to be eliminated. Nature abhors a vacuum, so these negative memes will resurface in the individual unless they are replaced by positive memes. The set of simple positive memes in Chapter Four which enhance remote viewing should be practised until they are habitual. Positive memes also reduce the basal level of the stress neurohormones and their associated electrical activity in the psiops investor, enabling the person to remain in the theta state all day. This results in augmented performance, that enables the remote viewing investor to control their reaction to stress, such that they thrive in an environment that would make normal people physical and mental wrecks. The end result of this is that the signal-to-noise ratio of remote viewing was increased significantly, with an investor that can eat up stress, out-think and outlast their competitors.

Business implications of psiops

Organisations can use remote viewing research on optimising human potential to dramatically increase the efficiency of their core business. Psiops is dependant on altering the state of brain function in the operator. This knowledge has a much more general application and leads to increased efficiency in mental processes. This means that staff who take psiops training are much more efficient at their jobs. An organisation that has better-functioning staff than its competitors can thrive even in the chaotic times that are now the norm.

Understanding of physiological processes in the brain and memetics (the theory of memes and their propagation) also leads to a revolution in the way we manage businesses. Treating staff in a way that optimises their potential leads to dramatic increases in profitability and the creation of organisations that can operate in real-time.

Investors who apply these techniques will find they can think more clearly, have advanced intuition and can model the future more accurately. This will make them better able to excel in making a fortune in the money markets. Further to this, remote sensing can be used as a very powerful psychic scanning tool to get into the mind of the market makers.

An organisation that uses psiops can drastically cut the absence rate of personnel, as well as reducing the stress and anxiety which overload our systems and which perpetually afflict modern man. This technology can cause a marked improvement in physiological and mental functioning, as a by-product of remote viewing training. This, as mentioned before, is because remote viewing phenomena are only allowed when the brain is in a quiescent state, which is only normally found in deep meditative states. By boosting the abilities of the personnel in their company, the psi-investor can maximise the profitability of his portfolio of investments. Psi-able staff can enable the investor to operate in more areas of the market, more efficiently.

RS protocols for the investor

1. As an introductory exercise you should relax. In your mind's eye, imagine your awareness fixated on your brain. Visualise the three different areas of the brain.

2. Visualise your biophysical field becoming stronger and 'soaking' into the brain, linking with the neural nets by use of calcium release at the synapse. This process primes the biophysical fields to interact with your brain on a higher level than morphogenetic effects.

3. Visualise an energy field which overlays your body, the biophysical field that is contiguous with your physical being. This technique of visualising the biophysical field is very important, in that it is used to programme the specific brain centres for remote sensing. Biophysical fields carry information and they can be programmed just like a computer.

4. Mechanism of RS. We can change all aspects of our performance, thus enabling us to have the edge over all our competitors. To enter the mindset of a market maker so we can get a good idea of how the market will behave, the first step is to list the perceptual cues we get when we try and remotely sense the market maker of interest. For business people, entering the mindset of a competitor may be more profitable.

5. As a next exercise, imagine the market maker of interest. Keep repeating this distant visualisation of the market maker. This exercise trains your biophysical awareness to remotely sense other people. It also raises the biophysical awareness from morphogenetic field functions to primary awareness. In plain language, you are training your biophysical fields into becoming aware of those of other people that you find of interest.

6. Start training your biophysical awareness to visualise the market maker speaking, in his and your mind's eye, giving you all the information you are interested in. This form of psychic interrogation was used by the US remote viewers when they wished to scan for information.

Remote influencing for the investor

An example of using remote influencing to obtain the desired stock movement might be visualising a market maker and remotely influencing them to buy a large volume of the stock you wish to go up, or sell a large volume if you wish it to go down. When you release this meme, since it is a biophysical thought-form, it will travel to the market maker and will plant the idea in his head that he must carry out this stock movement. This form of remote influencing is used subconsciously by men and women who are successful in the money markets. The biophysical field is well equipped to remotely influence people so that they are motivated by greed to buy stock or fear to sell stock. The expertise comes in directing which stock they buy or sell respectively.

Remote influencing is impossible to block if it is of this

high order. Many men and women have been drawn to buy stock they did not like at first glance. The remote influencing of the market maker overcame their normal consciousness and planted the meme for greed within their biophysical field, where it grew like a virus until it overcame their own will. This form of remote influencing has been honed by millions of years of evolution. Mankind is drawn to wealth and the power of money memes is second to none in the hierarchy of influences in humans. Market makers radiate this form of meme, which is fed power by the adaptive energy of their devoted acolytes. These money icons become centres of the money memes and normally become richer and richer using the life-force of the people who follow their trends.

For the normal male or female, bereft of the money meme, remote influencing can be used to coerce the money makers to buy or sell to their profit. The market makers become telepathically hypnotised and controlled in their investing, which benefits the remote influencer, who now know which stock is going up and which is going down.

For those of you wishing to use this form of market remote influencing the following protocols will prove of use:

1. Relax into the theta state by using the advanced relaxation protocols for interacting with the brain stress system.

2. Place your epicentre of attention on the thalamus brain centre, the organ of attention in the limbic system.

3. Use the mental laser of DA to draw the mental cinema screen in a clockwise direction in your mind's eye.

4. Send your remote viewing biophysical field to the target market maker you wish to remotely influence.

5. Focus your biophysical field on the pleasure centre in their brain.

6. Pulse the image of your stock at this brain centre in the target to be and command their brain to receive a sexual orgasm as the image of this stock is fed into their conscious, subconscious and unconscious.

7. Visualise a meme which commands that person to become besotted with the stock appearing on their mental screen.

8. Broadcast this meme into the biophysical field of the market maker. Once it has locked on to their brain, biophysical field and adaptive energy, it will feed on their sexual energy, flooding their mind with sexy images of your stock. This meme will feed on their adaptive energy, and makes them totally besotted with that stock. As more people learn the power of psi, these techniques of remote influencing become more and more powerful as the PDF loses all vestiges of control over human reality. With market remote influencing, the PDF has little control because humans have developed the power to remotely influence for money, or die out.

If you wish to use this form of market remote influencing to lower a stock price, the following protocols will prove of use. Follow steps 1 to 5 above, then:

6. Pulse the image of your stock at this brain centre in the

target to be and command their brain to receive a pain as the image of this stock is fed into their conscious, subconscious and unconscious.

7. Visualise a meme which commands that person to become fearful of that stock as it appears on their mental screen.

8. Broadcast this meme into the biophysical field of the market maker. At the same time, refocus your biophysical field on the amygdala while you pulse the image of your stock at this brain centre in the target, commanding their brain to receive a sensation of fear as the image of your stock is fed into their conscious, subconscious and unconscious. This enables your meme to access their energy. Once it has locked on to their brain, biophysical field and adaptive energy, it will feed on their energy – flooding their mind with fear images of your stock. This meme will feed on their adaptive energy and makes them totally fearful of that stock. This is how bear markets come into being.

ELEVEN

PSIOPS APPLICATIONS: A SUMMARY

Psiops automatically lowers the brain rhythms of managers participating in RV courses, so not only do the managers have enhanced intuition and the ability to enter their competitors' minds, but they can also out-think their foreign competitors. This enhanced mentation is a direct result of lowered basal EEG brain rhythms. Put simply, psiops technology-trained managers do not have their brains bathed in stress-inducing neurohormonal chemicals that are more appropriate for flight response. Their brains are also free from the incessant buzz of electrical over-stimulation that degrades clear thinking and decision making. They are not so stressed-out that they cannot think, which is the norm in most organisations. Having an organisation that can think properly when all your competitors cannot gives the psi-investor's company a commanding advantage.

Rather than putting these managers to sleep, this stress-reduced mental environment enables them to think with the use of less energy, so they have increased reserves of stamina and are not drained at the end of a long working day. Further to this, mentation that uses less energy enables these managers to run much larger mental simulations of what is going on in their business, its environs and the world milieu. Coupled with remote viewing, and sensing, this enables remote viewing trained managers to work in real-time, so they can instantly react to events. They can also increase the accuracy of their predictions, and home in on microclimates of opportunity.

An organisation that has psiops managers within it will find after a time that all staff begin to copy the enhanced performance psiops managers. The company culture will become suffused with a whole new range of psiops memes that will enable the company to work in real-time and enhance its profitability. Managers and staff will find they are fitter and suffer from less stress and they begin to enjoy their new enhanced efficiency.

Organisations that become the centre for these psiops memes will discover in staff an increase in mental powers and reduction in psychosomatic disease caused by stress. RS by managers of competitors to boost investment success or, conversely, to RS staff to feel how best to motivate them – will give the managers a tremendous advantage over their competitors in the marketplace.

Managers who can enter the mindset of staff will recognise problems developing before they crop up and harm the efficiency of the organisation. They will also recognise their own failings by remotely sensing staff concern about their performance. Motivational drives by managers will be successful if psiops is used to get into the mindset of the company culture, to really see what drives it and what holds it back. Knowledge of the destructive feedback cycle prevalent in organisations and personnel enables this malign software and set of memes to be removed from mental functions and the company culture.

Just eliminating the negative feedback cycle from an

organisation and its human personnel will dramatically increase productivity. All your competitors will still be wasting time and energy on this parasitic mental software and set of malign memes. Psiops also lowers the stress levels of staff, so they can out-think and outlast any competitor. The end result of this can be almost miraculous improvements in company culture, staff and managerial performances and the development of an organisation that dominates all aspects of its core competency

In conclusion, it can be seen that remote viewing technologies have a useful role to play in improving the way people work together within organisations. In the case of remote viewing, the swords to ploughshares idea, espoused after the Cold War ended, can really work. Military personnel may still be using remote viewing to spy on their enemies, but for the man on the street, psiops research can make you more productive and competitive, meaning better job security. It is strange how research into such arcane areas as remote viewing could show us so much about how people and organisations can improve the way they function. The psiops investor can boost his profits by using psiops, enabling an increase in the percentage of correct investments he or she makes.

Maybe other 'X-File' technologies contain similar keys to unlocking human potential and improving business. If there are so many benefits to be accrued for us all, let us hope the military release more revelations about the real X-Files in the near future. The business and investment worlds may never be the same again, now we have entered the age of psiops management and the coming psi-revolution.

GLOSSARY

adaptive energy   The body's biophysical energy used to empower the immune system, fight internal and external stressors and uphold the structural integrity of the body and mind.

algorithms   The step-by-step series of mathematical operations which computers use to process data.

behavioural kinesiology   The technique of manipulating the life-force by channelling this energy effectively around the body and destroying energy blockages. It consists of muscle testing to see the level of energy in the thymus and every other part of the body; pressure on energy blockage points to release life-force flows – so-called meridians – and to pump up the system from the thymus life-force battery. The author has taken it further by finding out ways of charging the thymus with life-force using the techniques of RS and RI, which have led to the development of psychotronic amplifiers to superboost it.

bilocation   The highly developed form of remote viewing in which the psychic viewer sees the target location as if actually there. A form of lucid dreaming (while awake).

biophysical awareness   The consciousness associated with the biophysical field (see below).

biophysical field   The energy body around the physical form which can be detached from the human body and used for remote viewing. Composed of fields unknown in the West. Includes morphogenetic fields (see below).

brain stress system   This is comprised of the *locus coeruleus* in the reptilian brain, the limbic system, the pituitary and adrenal glands. It initiates the fight-or-flight mechanism, while controlling the intensity of reaction mediated by hormones and neuroelectrical impulses.

CIA (Central Intelligence Agency)   A branch of the US intelligence service.

cinema method   The use of a mental cinema screen to receive information broadcast from the biophysical fields when remote viewing. Fixes attention on a 'TV image' which we are conditioned to watch.

CRV (co-ordinated remote viewing)   A technique of psychic viewing invented by Ingo Swann. Map co-ordinates are used to enable a trained remote viewer, in a state of normal consciousness, to give precise information on that location using a set of specialised protocols.

delta state   The state of consciousness normally experienced while in deep sleep, where your awareness is in its silent mode, directly accessing the unconscious.

DIA (Defence Intelligence Agency)   A branch of the US military involved with intelligence gathering.

directed attention   A focused, relaxed state of mind, centred on one specific function – remote viewing – and a tool to switch off internal chatter by use of the cinema method. A mental laser of attention emanating from the thalamus used to command and control psi-operations.

EEG (electroencephalograph)   A device which is used to record brain waves.

ELF (extremely low frequency waves)   This form of wave penetrates the skull and is the set of frequencies that the brain uses in behaviour. Therefore, ELF signals are used on microwave carrier waves to influence the behaviour of, make ill, or even kill high-profile people. Routinely used by British intelligence services.

entropy   A function of chaos: the more entropy, the greater the chaos.

epicentre of attention   The place the 'I' part of your mind inhabits. It is recreated to conform to reality so the 'I' part of you can perceive itself and perform optimally inside or outside of your body.

ERV (extended remote viewing)   An advanced form of psychic spying in which the clairvoyant descends into the theta state of consciousness, from which accurate psychic viewing can be established by following a special set of protocols.

ESP (extra sensory perception)   The ability to use psychic sensory means to read minds, see into the future or to remotely view distant locations.

group perception or *common consensus*   The perception of reality agreed upon by the group, which is not necessarily correct and very limiting.

group reality   The picture of reality the group takes to be the absolute truth but is in fact only a construct – a list of what is thought possible and what is not.

high-order consciousness   A heightened state of self-awareness, eg when the biophysical field is aware of itself.

meme   A contagious idea that spreads through the population; a biophysical field that is contagious. The term was first coined by Dr Richard Dawkins.

mental biofeedback   Using the mind to initiate changes in the body.

mental feedback loop   Conscious thought is redirected back onto itself to fixate thoughts on one idea group. In this case fixating attention on mental activity, or perception of reality.

morphogenetic field   The biophysical field used by the developing embryo to tell genes in cells to differentiate into different cell types, such as eye cells or hair cells. Cell development is controlled by these morphogenetic fields.

negative entropy   Order and structure.

oncogenes   These are genes that, when activated, cause cancer by producing tumour-inducing proteins.

PDE (the paranormal damping effect)   A creation of negative memes and meme structures which is used to suppress all paranormal abilities, to make agreed-upon things and events real, while strongly exorcising events and phenomena that do not agree with the common consensus.

primary consciousness   Being aware of one's environment.

precognition   Foreknowledge of the future through extrasensory means.

PRV (precognitive remote viewing)   The ability to use psychic viewing to see what may occur in the future.

psi   The use of psychic energy. Overall term encompassing remote viewing, remote influencing, psychotronics and all psychic ability.

psi fields   A class of fields discovered by Russian military scientists and include, according to their terminology, tarsionic, scalionic and leptionic fields.

psychotronics   The Russian research on the use of psi-energy to effect people and influence reality. Also included are Soviet research on mind control using psi and electromagnetic carrier waves for ELF signals.

RI (remote influencing)   The use of telepathic hypnotism to plant thoughts in another person's mind, to control that person's thoughts, or to cause bodily changes.

RK (remote killing)   The advanced application of psi that enables high-level operators to telepathically influence the brain of the victim to give them a heart attack, or to use telekinesis to rupture capillaries in the victim's brain to cause a stroke. Advanced remote influencing can switch on suicide genes in the victim.

RS (remote sensing)   The ability to psychically scan other people to telepathically sense what condition their body is in, or to begin to read thoughts and emotions running through their brain.

RV (remote viewing)   The facility to use clairvoyance to psychically view distant locations.

scanning   The military use of remote sensing to psychically interrogate the brain of the victim to gain information by ESP and telepathy.

schuman resonance   The natural frequency at which the planet resonates: 7.82 Hz.

shaman   A holy man of northern Asia in touch with spirits; also a medicine man.

signal-to-noise ratio   A method of determining the accuracy of remote viewing information; reproducing exactly what you see (signal) without any attempt at interpretation (noise).

situational awareness   The use of all the senses, especially vision, to build an accurate 3D-construct of all that is around you; called 'being in the clue' by fighter pilots, for whom it is an imperative.

suprameme   The collection of memes which rule each person's life.

telekinesis   Psychokinesis.

telomeres   Non-coding genetic material on the ends of the chromosomes which become smaller as the cell divides. When the telomere is finally terminated by successive truncations, the cell stops dividing and eventually dies.

tesla-level   When in the tesla-level, the psiops adept learn how to function in a state of lucid waking in the theta state, normally used for dreaming. By learning how to remotely sense one's inner self in the theta state, one gains intense clarity of thought and reasoning as well as significantly boosted cognitive and visio-spatial abilities normally only found in dreamers. Therefore, by learning how to make use of the dreaming state for conscious activity, one can use its eidectic (or photographic) memory and superfast computing abilities to vastly enhance one's capacities.

thymus and *thymus thump*   The thymus is the gland which stores biophysical energy – life-force – which vivifies the body. Lightly tapping the thymus is called the 'thymus thump', which, in concert with the intent to release this life-force from the thymus, gives the body an energy boost. Dr Mark Diamond MD, an American doctor, discovered this technique.

total order   A state of affairs in which chaos is an absolute minimum and order is the rule.

total reality   The true nature of things stripped free of preconceptions and unfiltered by programming in the brain. Influencing matter and mind – other people's brain functions by the power of the mind.

BIBLIOGRAPHY AND FURTHER READING

Bibliography

Brown, C (1997) *Cosmic Voyage*, Hodder & Stoughton, London

Ebon, M (1983) *Psychic Warfare: Threat or Illusion?*, McGraw-Hill, New York

Emerson, S (1988) *Secret Warriors Inside the Covert Military Operations of the Reagan Era*, Putnam, New York

Gris, H and Dick, W (1979) *The New Soviet Psychic Discoveries: A First-hand Report on the Latest Breakthroughs in Russian Parapsychological Research*, Souvenir Press, London

Houck, J (1993) 'Researching Remote Viewing and Psychokinesis', *TREAT V Conference Proceedings*, New Mexico (also available online at www.urigellar.com/content/research/houck1.htm)

Marrs, J (1997) *Alien Agenda*, HarperCollins, London

Morehouse, D (1996) *Psychic Warrior: Inside the CIA's Stargate Program*, St Martin's Press, New York

Ostrander, S and Schroeder, L (1971) *Psychic Discoveries Behind the Iron Curtain*, Prentice Hall, Englewood Cliffs, New Jersey

Ostrander, S and Schroeder, L (1997) *Psychic Discoveries:*

The Iron Curtain Lifted, Souvenir Press, London

Puthoff, H and Targ, R (1977) *Mind Reach*, Delacorte, New York

Ravenscroft, T (1987) *The Spear of Destiny*, Samuel Weiser

Rejdak, Z (1997) *Psychic Discoveries Behind the Iron Curtain Revealed*, Souvenir, London

Sagan, C (1997) *The Demon-haunted World: Science as a Candle in the Dark*, Ballantine Books, New York

Schnabel, J (1997) *Remote Viewers: The Secret History of America's Psychic Spies*, Dell, New York

Schroeder, L and Ostrander, S (1979) *Superlearning*, Souvenir, London

Smith, C and Best, S (1989) *Electromagnetic Man*, St Martin's Press, New York

Swann, I (1986) 'Coordinate Remote Viewing', www.crvmanual.com/manual/1.html

Vasiliev, L (1962) *Experimental Research of Mental Suggestion*, University Press, Leningrad

Author's publications

Rifat, T (2001) *Remote Viewing: What It Is, Who Uses It and How To Do It, Vision Paperbacks, London*

(1997) 'A remote view of Delenn – from *Babylon 5*,' *Sightings*, **2** (3)

(1997) 'Alien mind war – psychic warfare', *Alien Encounters* (13), summer

(1997) 'Changing your mind – mind control', *Alien Encounters* (11), May

(1997) 'Exploring the megaverse', *Enigma* (4)

(1997) 'It's all in the mind', *Enigma*, February/March

(1997) 'Losing your mind! Mind control technology', *Sightings* (12)

(1997) 'Mind control – Big Brother is all in the mind', *UFO Reality* (8), June/July

(1997) 'Mind wars – Big Brother is out to get you', *Enigma* (6)

(1997) 'Quantum leap – remote viewing', *Sightings* (9)

(1997) 'Watching the watchers – remote viewing', *Alien Encounters*, December

(1996–97) 'Remote viewing – the ESP of ESPionage', *Nexus*, October/November/December/January/ February/March

(1996) 'Remote viewing – Why *The X-Files* is good for business', *Enigma*, December

Further reading

Adams, J (1995) 'Day of the Pentagon mindbenders', *The Sunday Times*, 3 December

Anderson, J and Binstein, M (1995) 'Psychic spies have a home at the CIA', *United Features* syndicate, 1 November

Constantine, A (1996) *Psychic Dictatorship in the USA*, Feral House, Portland, Oregon

Dennett, D (1996) *Darwin's Dangerous Idea: Evolution and the Meanings of Life*, Simon and Schuster, New York

Dowbenko, U (1997) 'True adventures of a psychic spy – an interview with David Morehouse', *Nexus*, August/September/ October/November

Edelman, G (1988) *Neural Darwinism: The Theory of*

Neuronal Selection, Basic Books, New York

Fleming, M (1995) 'Psychic soldier sells his bizarre tale to Hollywood', *Variety*, November

Goodwin, B (1994) *How The Leopard Changed Its Spots*, Weidenfeld and Nicholson, London

Hameroff, S, Kaszniak, A and Scott, A (1996) *Toward a Science of Consciousness, The First Tucson Discussions and Debates*, MIT Press, Boston, Massachusetts

Keith, J (1993) *Secret and Suppressed*, Feral House, Portland, Oregon

Matthews, R (1996) 'CIA signed up psychics as spooks', *Sunday Telegraph*, 4 August

Penrose, R (1989) *The Emperor's New Mind*, Oxford University Press, Oxford

Rickard, B (1996) 'From Russia with anxiety', *Fortean Times*, **87**, June

Utts, J (1995) 'Scientific verification of RV', *The Journal of Scientific Exploration*, Stanford, **10** (1), pp I–III

Vistica, G (1995) 'Psychics and spooks', *Newsweek*, 11 December

Wolf, J (1995) 'Psychic power real, but not good for spying, CIA says', *Reuters*, 28 November; ISCNI Flash, 1 Dec 1995

ABOUT THE AUTHOR

Tim Rifat is Europe's leading expert on remote viewing-psychic spying, psi-warfare, mind control and microwave weaponry. As the only independent scientist in the field, he has published numerous articles and books, including *Remote Viewing* (Vision Paperbacks 2001).

He runs psiopsmanagement.com – the most comprehensive remote viewing training business in Europe. His website is www.psiopsmanagement.com.